Monsters Are Alive

By Steve Preston

1st Edition

© Copyright 2015, Steve Preston

Table of Contents

Introduction

Every once in a while we hear stories about monsters that have been found around the world. Easily discarded, there are issues concerning ignoring the obvious. If people see things, there might be things to see. This is especially true today when amateur video captures creatures thought never to exist or ones that were thought to be extinct. This book traces animals existence that we may call monster from the time of the Titans who ruled the Earth and dinosaurs walked, through the time of the ancient Heaven war and the monsters that were created to help fight in that war. Continuing forward in time we will look at the monsters of the ANAK people. We find that many prehistoric animals were still alive during the Pleistocene Age. We are told many people and animals died as a result of the great Pleistocene Extinction and worldwide flood. What we find is many of the so-called extinct animals were still alive or re-made after this horror and up until fairly recent time images of massive creatures for drawn, etched, modeled, and described around the world. We find a massive increase in civilization and science up until 3100BC after the worst war of modern times destroyed 1/3 of the world population by one reference. The time was called Zep-Tepi by the Egyptians, and the new Age of Kali by the Indians. Over in the new world, the PreMaya started a brand new 5000 year calendar and the Mongulala of Brazil called it a New Age. Whatever happened, it seems genetic science had been destroyed and mankind had been set back to a quasi-Stone Age existence for a time. The reason I'm am explaining these things is that some of the marvelous creatures created before this time survived the War and procreated. Instead of finding all dinosaur like creatures dead 5500 years ago. Some seem to have survived.

Generally the book is divided into the time periods listed below.

The Mesozoic Monsters--- Those that evolved or were manufactured during the Age of the Dinosaurs and generally became extinct during the Cretaceous Extinction.

The Pleistocene Monsters--- Those who were re-established during the Triassic and Pleistocene Age.

The Holocene Monsters- Those who were re-established after the Pleistocene Extinction and described in many of the ancient histories as being alive during post extinction times.

Recent Monsters- Those that have been spotted recently.

Additionally each section is subdivided by area of witness including the Jewish, Sumerian, Babylonian, Assyrian, Chinese, Indian, Egyptian, Mayan, and other civilizations. Before we can get started, we need to first change the way we think about when dinosaurs were roaming the earth. To understand when they were here we need to know something about radio-active decay timing.

Radio-Active Decay Timing

If the distance from the Earth to the Sun stays constant, the Sun activity is regulated, no nuclear events occur on or near earth, or things don't get abnormally hot or cold, radioactive materials decay at what seems to "generally" be a constant rate. Just count neutrons and everything goes into place, but things have not been so constant. When we say radio-active decay timing, we do not simply mean Carbon 14 dating. People have gotten so used to believing in carbon 14 markers that they don't even realize that extending the timing beyond 4 or 5 thousand years really is dangerous. Here are a few of the nuclear decay materials and methods currently being used to inaccurately time things.

- Carbon 14 percent timing
- Thermo-luminescence Testing
- Electronic Spin Resonance Dating
- Fission Track Dating
- Ocean Sediment Testing
- Thorium Protactinium Dating
- Argon-argon Dating
- Lead, Lead, Lead Testing

To work, all expect radio-active decay to be constant. Unfortunately, we now know it is not.

Radio-Active Solar Flare Variation

The majority of geologists today tell you that radiometric dating has narrowed the age of Earth to about 4.5 billion years, give or take a couple of percent. We now know that is hogwash and are refining the timing more and more each day. The Earth and everything in it is much younger. Researchers at Purdue and Stanford have found evidence that radio decay rates are not constant at all. On December 13, 2006, a magnificent solar flare flung radiation and solar particles toward Earth. Measuring the decay rate of manganese-54 during the flare proved to be very interesting as the decay rate dropped during the time of the radiation fallout. It was determined that solar neutrinos zipped through space and affected Mn-54's decay rates used in the experiment. Just think about this. They were testing a single solar flare event and the change was significant. The sun has these things all the time.

Seasonal Variation

It was also found that the decay rates of silicon-32 and radium-226 showed seasonal variation, according to data collected at Brookhaven National Laboratory on Long Island and the Federal Physical and Technical Institute in Germany. This error was just the material sitting there with almost no outside interference.

Just Plane Different

Wood buried in igneous rock in Queensland Australia has been dated to 40 thousand years, while the basalt around it dated to 45 million years. Both dating subjects should have given the same date, since the igneous rock was formed at the same time the wood was buried. Many of the "data-ologists" don't tell you about major errors like this.

Lava Errors

Excess argon-36 was found in three out of 26 lava flows in recent times. So Argon/argon testing would show a much older date that actually was "KNOWN" This is believed to be because there was too much of the argon-36 in the first place. In the Grand Canyon lava flow testing showed lower levels of lava were younger than the top layers. At different volcano sites, that had eruption in 1949, 1954 and 1975. The same thing was noted These samples were dated by Geochron Laboratories of Cambridge, Massachusetts. Even though the oldest of these samples are just over sixty-years old, the lab tests provided ages that ranged from 270,000 years to 3.5 million years old. Additionally, we go to Mt. St. Helens and its eruptions in the 1980's. Samples there gave old ages in the range of 300,000 to 2.7 million years. Hopefully, you are beginning to see that we know less about how old we are than you believed before reading this.

Distance to the Sun

8

If neutrinos from a single solar flare can make things look older, what if the entire Earth was closer to the sun? I know that sounds odd, so just keep it in the back of your mind right now as we look at Ice Core Testing. I'll be getting back to the sun distance in a while.

Ice Core Dating

The chart below shows ice core data from Antarctica presented earlier. What we see is that after 400 thousand years ago, there are very distinct and abrupt thermal changes every 100 thousand years or so. The cyclic nature continues before that time, but the events are greatly softened showing the characteristics of the Earth were hugely different before that fateful time. It is as if the planet changed its size as the massive area lost when the Pacific Ocean was carved out. After that time the smaller earth could have more extreme climate and effluent density changes. Please don't worry that you were told the Pacific Ocean was scooped out 212 million years ago as we look deeper.

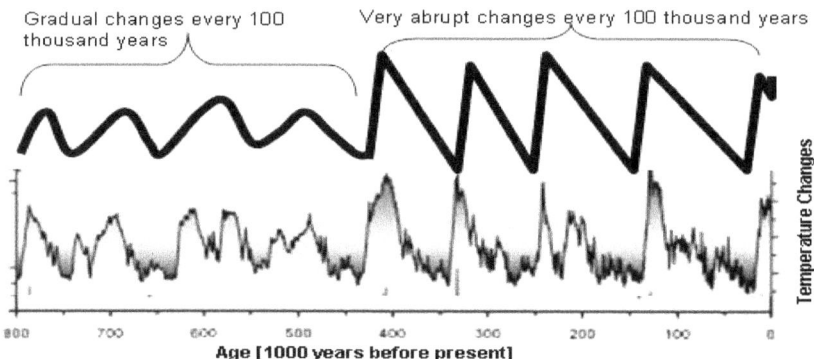

Although the task is tedious, ice can be examined just like tree rings. Each summer ice changes its consistency. $H_2O(16)$ is more concentrated in the summer while $H_2O(18)$ is more concentrated in the winter. This gives us indication to the level of CO_2 which in turn allows us to understand something about the temperature levels. As the yearly cycle has freezing and thawing, ice consistency varies each day, seasonally, and yearly, depending on Earth axis and other critical elements. Anyway, scientists around the world started boring holes in ice. The most coring is done in Greenland and Antarctica. The sample below stops 400 thousand years ago.

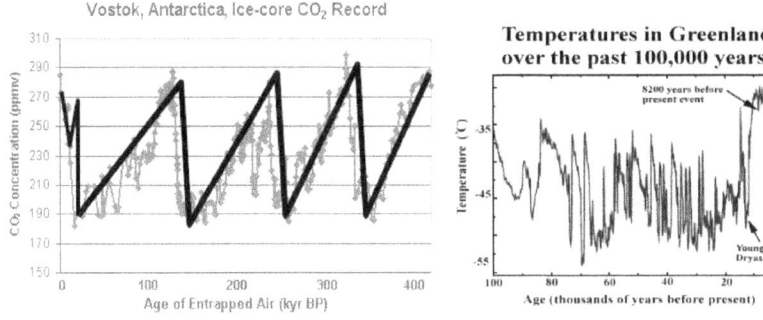

Vostok, Antarctica, Ice-core CO₂ Record

Temperatures in Greenland over the past 100,000 years

Notice, every 100 thousand or so years, there is a MASSIVE change in the CO2 concentration or temperature associated to some massive change, especially when we find that only about 2% of the airborne CO2 even reaches the ground. One would think this type of massive change would kill animals, so we might be able to use the Ice core to give us a different timeline that is better characterized by physical evidence around the world. Please notice a shape rise about 11000 years ago and then a second one 10 thousand years ago signaling the Pleistocene extinction.

Greenland Check

From the next chart, we can see a correlation in near term events. 11 thousand years ago a major spike in temperature with a fast cooling followed by another just a thousand years later then an almost flat plateau where Greenland's temperature has not changed and Greenland's position relative to the axis of spin has been unchanged. Before that time, it seems, the temperature was generally colder with what looks like a rise in temperature starting around 100 thousand years ago. Generally both Ice core columns show identical timing.

Paleo-Magnetics

We all know the Atlantic Ocean is getting wider about an inch a year, averaged worldwide. While the building of the great mountains has little to do with the normal tectonic plate "drift" We can pretty accurately measure the widening ocean in various ways including measuring distances between matched magnetic landmarks on either side of a widening gap on the ocean floor. The Old theory indicated that 180 million years ago the continent Pangea began splitting apart and has been drifting ever since. In so doing, the landmasses of the Western and Eastern hemispheres separated and opened the Atlantic Ocean basin today.

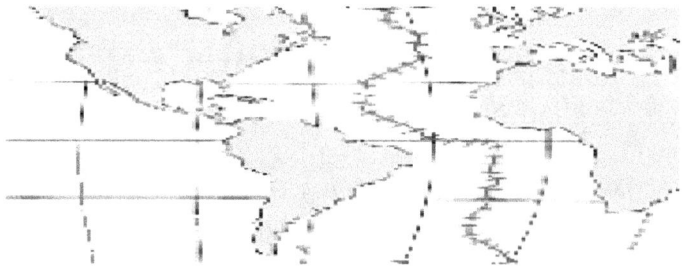

Plate tectonics tells us the outer hard crust of Earth consists actually of a dozen or so distinct, hard plates that drift individually on hot, deformable rock. An unequal distribution of heat within Earth moves the plates. The boundary between the plates forming the Atlantic Ocean is smack down the middle along the Mid-Atlantic Ridge, shown as the hashed line in the figure to the right. The ridge is where we must look to find a widening gap, which accounts for the widening ocean. That is where we measure the rate of separation. Where the plates separate, white-hot soft mantle oozes up from great depths within the Earth to fill the gap. The molten rock cools slowly into new slivers of sea floor. This happened over and over again through the eons. That's how the Atlantic Ocean widened-by a spreading sea floor. We measure the gap rate in various ways including direct measurements of plate movement using satellite images. Another is the Paleo-magnetic method. As the Earth's magnetic poles reverse polarity periodically, the North Pole becomes the South Pole and vice versa and much of the magma spewing out is iron.

Iron-rich rock has a peculiar property: heat it above its curie point of 580 degrees Centigrade and it loses its magnetism. When it cools the rock gets re-magnetized in the direction of the existing Earth's magnetic field. So it's a magnet with the poles aligning with the poles of the Earth at the time of the cooling. The neat thing about this is: the magnetic field of the rock, once cooled, stays frozen in this orientation. It becomes a record of the Earth's field at the time of its cooling. To measure the rate of separation, we identify two slivers of sea floor on opposite sides of the ridge that have the same magnetic polarities frozen at the same time. If you know when these reversals occur, one can simply measure the distance between magnetic alignments of the ocean floor and one can determine the rate of expansion and how long ago Pangea began to separate. Unfortunately, if the initial time-base is wrong everything is skewed.

With that, let's look at the center of the Atlantic Ocean. The graph following shows the last 14 flips over recent times. Using mathematical models of the external crust and inner molten material, researchers have estimated with mathematic models that the Earth should flip and stabilize on its axis about every 100 thousand years. The problem with trying to determine the actual workings of the Earth is that no one has ever seen the inside of the Earth to model it properly, but the results do confirm the high possibility of a polar flip, which will cause mass destruction, tidal waves, and major climatic changes. With that scary introduction, let's look at the chart as it currently has been determined and match it up with the Ice Core samplings.

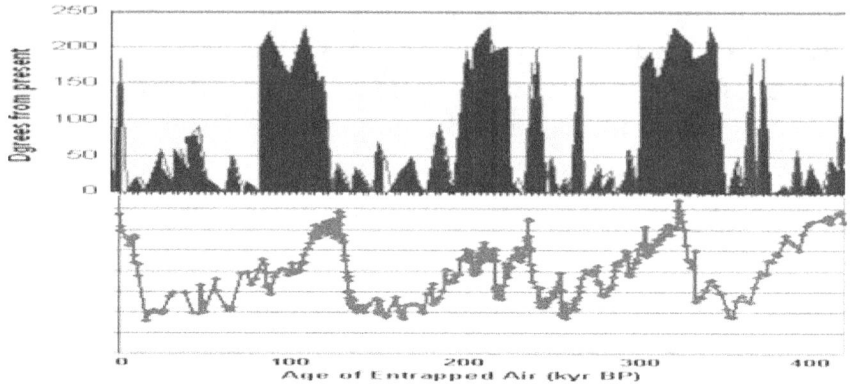

Changes in the earth axis seem to correlate very well with the data from the Ice core testing when the data is matched to the 100 thousand year match model. Here is what you should recognize. The magnetic field reversals and the cyclic ice core CO_2 levels seem to have a repetitive, cyclic nature. Even that strange change around 230 thousand years ago seems to correlate with the mid Atlantic data. I need you to notice one more thing. The compressed timing gives us more substantiation for 2 major climactic events occurring within only a very short period of time around 10 thousand and 11 thousand years ago.

Plate Shifts

Like the magnetic shifts, major crust movements or earth axis positional changes have been estimated to happen about every 20,000 years. The most recent ones occurred 43,000, 22,000, and 10,000 years ago. Sometimes the crust and magnetic field seems to wander over a number of years and other times it seems to jerk suddenly. One of the theories is that these "jerks in the crust are apparently caused by the uneven weight of the various plates supported on the surface of the Earth; especially the 19 quadrillion tons of mass called Antarctica which is located at the present day South Pole. Each time a movement occurs, terrible things happen like tropical areas turning into glaciers. Whether the evidence shows magnetic field wander or plate shift wander doesn't really matter, because the outcome is the same.

Tropical Arctic

14

Researchers have found evidence that the Arctic was tropical for a short time, 100 thousand years ago, or so. They found bones of early crocodiles, turtles and fish that were all tropical and estimated the summer temperatures reached into the 90s. This could only mean that the plates shifted or the planet axis moved by a substantial amount. Finds similar to this have convinced many that the outer core of the Earth moves continually and that the movement is in jerks over time.

Tropical Antarctic

If we move to the other side of the world, we find the same thing. Swamp type dinosaur bones have been found along with remains of plants that existed before parts of Antarctica became extremely cold [the last time]. It seems the animals found would have been on earth around 100 thousand years ago according to the new timing. With that little piece of data, let's look at a very special timeline track called Hawaii. Hawaii hasn't always been where it is today. A record of its travels shows up as something called hot spots.

Hot Spot Dating

If the axis is changing, there should be some dramatic physical evidence and there is. The evidence is not only from the magnetic field alignments of molten material in the Atlantic Ocean, but also some easily seen evidence. The evidence is in the form of hot spots. The best hot spot to discuss is Hawaii. The volcanic action in Hawaii has nothing to do with the edges of the plates. The picture on the following page shows the basic outlines of the major plates and these anomalous "Hot Spots". The hot spots don't stay still. They wander, but they wander in straight lines interrupted by abrupt turns. By measuring the distance the "hot spot" travels, we can determine how long the Earth or a particular plate on the Earth stayed with a particular axis of rotation. The hot spots wander because the inner core is much denser than the outer core, and occasionally the two slip in the direction perpendicular to the axis of rotation. The reason we know the slippage is perpendicular is that it is still happening.

Plate Movement Direction

If we look at the apparent trail of the Hawaiian Islands over time as shown below, a clear path is noted and times for each abrupt change has been approximated by distance. By the way, a new hotspot has just opened 73km south of the big island showing that the plate wander direction is still in the same direction as it has been over the last 10 thousand years and its perpendicular to the Earth rotational axis. With the distance between Midway and Hawaii known to be 1300 miles, the total distance of the hotspot track is about 4500 miles. New data has compressed the tack to agree with all the rest of the timing without the old nuclear decay standard. This makes the movement about 50 feet per year as shown below left.

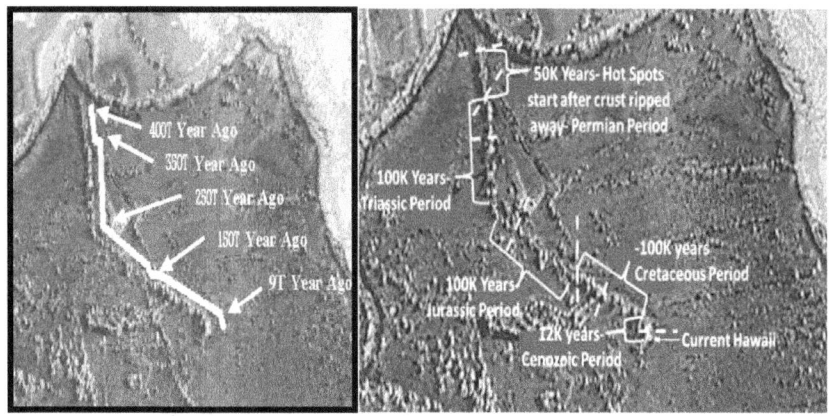

Initially this sounds inappropriate as the Atlantic only increase in size about 1 inch per year today, but the motion of the hotspot has little to do with the expansion of the Atlantic Ocean as it is characterized by the differential between the Earth inside spin and the outside spin.

More Detail-I know you are thinking this is interesting, but it doesn't really help too much. So we have correlation of other hot spot trails and what seems to be timing compression similar to others used in this new light, but can the hot spots be traced back to the Antarctic Ice core? The answer can be seen in the second graphic above. We know that the trails are produced perpendicular to the axis of rotation of the earth which is described as dotted lines below. If we that the changes in the earth axis at the apparent changes, we find something VERY interesting as shown next.

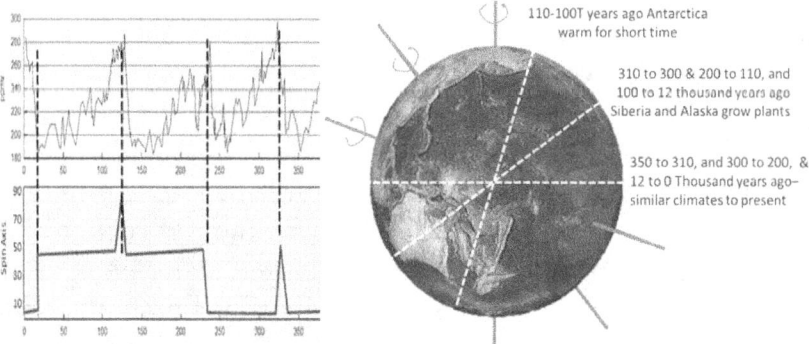

Notice that for a few thousand years about 100 thousand years ago Antarctica was probably warm between the Jurassic and

Cretaceous Period. Sure enough animals from that time have been found under the ice---just sitting there waiting to be found. The graphic above right tries to show some possible major earth "settling" points and general information about those spin axis's. For instance, notice that the earth spin goes along the east coast of the United States 11 thousand years ago. This will be important later as we piece all of this together to try to see critical time marks to help us reevaluate the time line for us as humans.

Some Don't Believe in Shifting Poles

Some people try to infer that this whole thing about the Earth changing its axis is hogwash. Well, I think that there is just way too much data to assume otherwise. Antarctica with its dinosaur bones, the quick frozen Mammoths, the various polarities of the deposited iron from volcanic action in the middle of the Atlantic Ocean; they all tell the same story. The Earth axis can move and with it there can be relatively fast and devastating climatic changes. These changes are horrible, but may not be the responsible party for most of the extinction periods. The most effective exterminator on the Earth has been and will continue to be the Comet or Meteor. Whenever a comet or meteors hit and the earth axis shifts right afterwards, total chaos occurs as it did about 100 thousand years ago then 11 thousand years ago followed by another attack 10 thousand years ago. These 3 dates are important to us as humans. A hundred thousand years ago makes the extinction of most of the dinosaurs and most of the human race at that time. After the extinction, the Bible indicated that the earth was without form and void so we can understand just how horrible it really was. Twelve thousand years ago was the last major earth axis shift and it quick froze mammoths eating in a field in Siberia when, all of a sudden, the landscape was almost immediately turned into a polar region where everything was dead. The Bible talks about this as being the destruction of the planet Rahab and other texts tell us 1/3 of the entire population of the earth was wiped out. Three thousand years later another attack temporarily shifted the earth melting the ice caps, forming massive tidal waves and drowning just about everything and everyone left on the earth. When the clamor had ended the earth

18

shifted back to its 11 thousand year alignment as captured in the mid-Atlantic magma and the Hawaiian hot spot trail and life began again.

While all this was going on, animals would die and on special occasions, they would fossilize. For decades, scientists have been using fossilization comparisons to date things, but there were problems. One was they kept finding giant people who lived with the dinosaurs. As the dinosaurs would walk along the beaches of that day, people would come one the same beaches. We believe they went to the beach at separate times, but both sets of footprints were fossilized together, most likely before the great extinction that ended the Cretaceous Period. I'll explain the "most likely" later. Right now it is important to understand just how unstable everything is and how the nuclear decay timing could get so messed up. This timeline is substantially compressed over what you normally see. Mainstream, well meaning, lazy, researchers pull old details of the development of the earth and mankind and provide a timeline similar to the one shown next.

Standard Geological Timeline

Era/Period/Epoch	Time (M Years ago)
Archaeozoic Period	5000-1500
Proterozoic Period	1500-545
Cambrian period	550-500
Ordovician period	500-440
Silurian period	440-410
Devonian period	410-365
Carboniferous period	365-300
Permian period	300-250
Triassic period	250-212
Jurassic period	212-145
Cretaceous period	145-65
Tertiary period	65-0.04
Pleistocene period	0.04-0.01
Holocene period	0.01-0

Wow! How neat. Hundreds of millions of years, and many, many long time periods show up to embellish our history and allow for a development timeline that allows for something we call evolution. I'm not saying evolution is bunk. There is no question that evolution is real and it caused many of the changes in characteristics of animals seen in ancient times and today. That being said, survival of the fittest, is not the reason for most of the adaptations and stretching out the timeline to allow for the level of absurdity is not called for. The main reason scientists have allowed themselves to go down the rabbit hole of the previous timeline is something called radioactive decay. Thought to be a constant and well documented, believable, unshaking truth, we now find out that many things change these constants tremendously.

More Probable Geological Timeline

A better timeline might be the one shown below. Instead of hundreds and hundreds of millions of years, the timeline looks like it must be compressed to be a hundredth of that originally described as unshakable. I know this sounds absurd to you right now, but, hopefully when you read about the proof, you will be less inclined to simply take for granted that you are being told the whole truth and investigate on your own. I am not saying my timeline is unshakable either, but it explains a lot to the anomalies typically being brushed over by those trying to control reality by decree.

Era/Period/Epoch	time (T years ago)
Archaeozoic period	50,000-3000
Proterozoic period	3000-1000
Cambrian period	1000-900
Ordovician period	900-800
Silurian period	800-700
Devonian period	700-600
Carboniferous period	600-500
Permian period [1st Mars event]	500-400
Triassic period [Pacific Ocean]	400-300
Jurassic period [Titan]	300-200
Cretaceous period [ANAK]	200-100
Tertiary period [Adam]	100-40
Quaternary period [Flood]	40-10
Holocene period [Present]	10-0

20

Titan Monsters

You might ask who were the titan people? You have heard about them in Greek Mythology and understood them to be fiction. Unfortunately for those wanting to believe that, it is simply not true. The titan, gigantic people living during ancient times, did live in a civilized world accompanied by the dinosaurs. As the majority of the dinosaurs became extinct at the end of the Cretaceous, we are talking about way back in time. While I'm not getting into the "normal" dinosaurs in any great detail, the ancient stories about the creation of these monsters will be addressed.

Evolutionist Dinosaurs

No one tells you how the huge things got here, but they do come up with some extremely odd theories that make almost no sense. The one I like is that a pool of special sugars were all deposited on the earth and some lightning came along and hit the right distance from this stuff to force the sugars in a complex alignment known as DNA. If that wasn't fanciful enough, another 4 or five lightning bolts hit nearby pool with just the right energy level to mix special sugars in different pools to make procreable DNA structures similar to the first. These DNS things somehow grew into amoeba and mistakes in regeneration finally cause d dinosaurs to simultaneously regenerate from the mistakes close enough to mate.

Creationist Dinosaurs

Another theory is that 6 thousand years ago God came down and went poof and all the animals in the world were here. God being mistake prone, made many, many mistake animals when he did this thing all at once and decided to call the animal mistakes the unclean animals [or abominable animals] and the ones that came out alright the clean or [acceptable] animals.

Intelligent Design Dinosaurs

Some go in between. Thinking God would not make mistakes, they think someone helped, but the initial life was created by an omniscient Creator God. We will look at some of the mistakes and writings to show that these mistakes were the actions of ancient people known as Titans by the Greeks and described in the book of Genesis as the Great Men of Old who were here well before the time of the Homo-Erectus man who was created during the Tertiary Period. Now that you have bought in totally that Titans went around making monsters during the Mesozoic Age, I won't have a problem convincing you of the rest of the stuff. For those not basking in the glow of understanding, let me give some more insight.

First Believe That Titan People Were Here

Before you can possibly believe that Titans monsters were created by Titans, I think we had better provide a tiny sampling of the hundreds of pieces of evidence that prove their civilized existence. So we have seen written testimony, but I'm thinking you are doubting the whole TITAN giants walking around during the time of Dinosaurs. I think it's important to show the beginnings of physical evidence suggesting a race of gigantic humans that lived millions of years ago. These were not savages, but civilized humans. One might think that if these titans made the dinosaur monsters, they probably walked with them. Our first stop is in the United States. Some of these characters were 20 feet tall and most of the footprints found show how these guys took off their shoes whenever they were on the beaches that allowed for reasonable fossilization. Luckily for us, when the dinosaurs came around the same beaches, we got their imprints.

Dinosaurs & Giants-Texas is full of sites – At this one 14 human and 134 dinosaur tracks have been found together and estimated to be over 70 million years old. [Next Left]

Another Texas Site- This one had 15 human prints near dinosaur print finds and was estimated to be over 70 million years old. This walking with dinosaurs seemed to be a common occurrence. [Next Right]

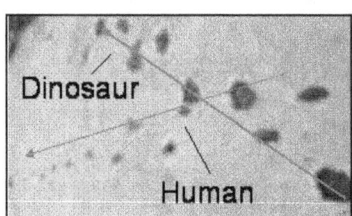
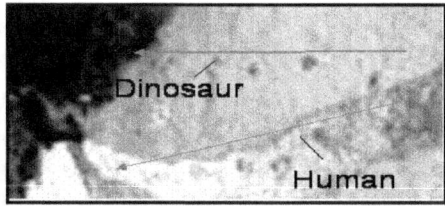

Texas 1976- Many human and dinosaur prints were found together at Glen Rose, Texas. In one instance, the dinosaur prints actually went over the top of one of the footprint impressions in a series. 203 dinosaur prints and 57 human prints were found in the same area. The largest human print was over 16 inches long. The prints have been estimated to be 70 million years old. The above ancient giant footprint was found near the main group. [Next left]

Here is still an example of the fantastic finds in Texas. This one was found in 1971 and is another example from Glen Rose. It shows a giant man going one way while a dinosaur was going the other. Lucky for the man, the footprint is huge [18 inches long]. Like the others, it is estimated age over 70 million years old. The man using that foot would have been over 12 foot tall. [Next Right]

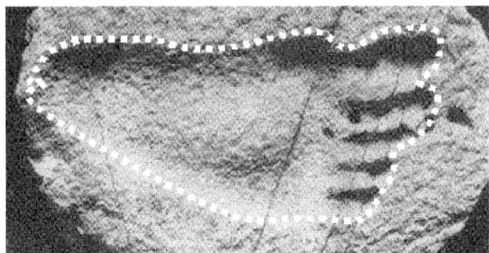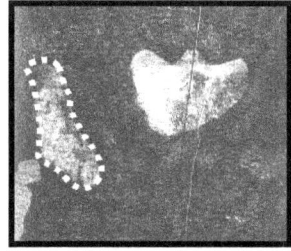

Illinois-1962-A human skeleton was found 90 feet below the surface in a coal seam and was reported in "The Geologist". The estimated age of the coal seam is in excess of 100 million years old.

California Titan- In 1833, soldiers digging a pit at Lompock Rancho, California unearthed a 12-foot tall giant with double rows of teeth, both on top and on the bottom. The Lompock giant's teeth, while unusual, were not unique. Another ancient skeleton, later found on Santa Rosa island off the coast of California, showed the same dental peculiarity. Other sites show similar ancient, completely upright walking humans. The following collage show some of the more famous petrified beach walks proving ancient humans went to the beach and that dinosaurs like the same beaches as humans.

Nevada Titan- In July, 1877, four prospectors were looking for gold and silver outcroppings in a desolate, hilly area near the head of Spring Valley, not far from Eureka, Nevada. One of the men spotted something peculiar projecting from a high ledge. The prospector was surprised to find a human leg-bone and knee cap sticking out of solid rock. He and his companions dislodged the oddity with picks. Realizing they had a most unusual find, the men brought it into Eureka, where it was placed on display. The stone in which the bones were embedded was a hard, dark red quartzite, and the bones themselves were almost black with carbonization showing its great age. When the surrounding stone was carefully chipped away, the specimen was found to be composed of a leg bone broken off four inches above the knee, the knee cap and joint, the lower leg bones, and the complete bones of the foot. Several medical doctors examined the remains, and indicated that they had indeed once belonged to a human being, and a very modern-looking one. But for us the best part was their size: From knee to heel they measured 39 inches. Their owner in life had thus stood over 12 feet tall. Compounding the mystery further was the fact that the rock in which the bones were found **dated to the era of the dinosaurs**, the Jurassic Era - over 185 million years old. The local papers ran several stories on the marvelous find, and two museums sent investigators to see if any more of the skeleton could be located. Unfortunately, nothing else but the leg and foot existed in the rock.

More Nevada- In 1947 a local newspaper reported the discovery of nine-foot-tall skeletons by amateur archeologists working in Death Valley. The archeologists involved also indicated that they had found what appeared to be the bones of tigers and dinosaurs with the human remains. There was an entire village of people living underground in Death Valley thousands of years ago, but that is another story.

Arizona Titan- In 1923, Mr. Samuel Hubbard discovered the remains of giants in the Grand Canyon of Arizona. The discovery consisted of the following: Petrified bodies of two human beings about 18 and 15 feet in height respectively. One of these was buried under a recent rock fall which required several days' work to remove. The other, of which Mr. Hubbard took photographs, was in a crevice and inaccessible. The bodies were formed from limestone petrifaction and embedded in sandstone millions of years ago.

More Arizona [1960s]- Tracks of a barefoot human child were found, alongside some dinosaur tracks. The location was the Moenkopi Wash, near the little Colorado River in northern Arizona. In 1984, similar tracks were found not far from the Moenkopi site. Many human tracks, dinosaur tracks, and a handprint of a child that had fallen. More adult tracks were found in 1986. The tracks were dated to be late Triassic to early Jurassic, some 100 to 175 million years old. In addition to 300 tridactyle dinosaur tracks, sheep tracks, bivalve prints, large amphibian and lungfish marks were found. Over 60 human tracks have been mapped and photographed at this location.

Colorado 1867-Human remains were found imbedded a silver vein at a depth of 400 feet Estimated age that the vein was formed was 135 million years ago.

Montana Bear Creek Report-In the Eagle three Cole mine at Bear Creek Montana in 1920 two human molars were found three times larger than normal. The coal had been a forest millions of years ago.

Titan Finds Around the World

The United States certainly wasn't the only place that our predecessors lived. They lived around the worlds. Here are a few of the finds of these extremely ancient ones.

Turkish Titan-In the late 1950's during road construction in Homs southeast Turkey, many tombs of Giants were unearthed. These tombs were 4 meters long, and when entered in 2 cases the human thigh bones were measured to be over 47 inches in length. It was calculated that the person who owned this Femur probably stood at fourteen to sixteen feet tall.

Soviet Union 1983-According to the "Moscow News", human footprints were found alongside and in the same strata as three toed dinosaur tracks. The estimated age is 80 million years old. While these humans may not have been giants, they must have had a giant amount of courage.

Puebla Mexico- Here, researchers have found many barefoot and shoed prints stuck in stone to show their antiquity. The picture above is one of many showing an ancient shoed visitor to this area some 50 million years ago. Some of these prints show giants lived in Puebla.

Mexico 1925-According to the Washington Post, June 22, 1925, and the New York Herald-Tribune, June 21, 1925, a mining party found skeletons measuring 10 to 12 feet, with feet 18 to 20 inches long, near Sisoguiche, Mexico. [Next]

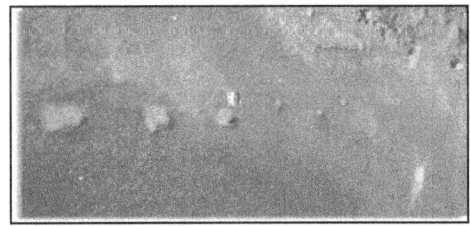

More Mexican Titans- According to a press clipping, dated Nayarit, Mexico, May 14, 1926- Capt. D. W. Page discovered the bones of a race of giants who averaged over ten feet in height. The Los Angeles Times, October 2, 1927- It indicated that *explorers in Mexico located large human bones near Tapextla, indicating a race of "gigantic size." El Boquin, on the Mico River- Press accounts said that the skeleton of a gigantic man, with head missing, was unearthed at El Boquin, on the Mico River, in the Chontales district. The ribs were a yard long and four inches wide and the shin bone was too heavy for one man to carry.* Now that is a giant.

Jurassic Human Skull-In 1993, a Peruvian newspaper reported that a human skull was discovered in. Jurassic rock in the Paracas National Reserve. The skull is shown in the following graphic next to a "modern skull, Note that it is almost exactly like modern man skull except larger. It was one we could call a Titan.

This is only a very small sampling. The titan evidence from Australia is awesome as shown below and around the world these Titans walked and worked. One of the jobs was biology and genetics. Their job was to create animals for work, pleasure and war.

Smart

These guys were just relaxing on the beach walking barefooted with dinosaurs, every year we find more and more about this ancient society procession nuclear materials in Gabon, Africa,

28

designing batteries found in California, Floors and walls seemingly "grown" in place, advanced metallurgy, and all types of consumer goods and hardware encased in Geodes or lumps of coal or inside layers of slate, etc. While this is not the topic of this book, we must wonder just how advanced this once great society really was.

Biblical References

First of all, we need to look in Genesis to see just who made the monsters according to the book Moses wrote 3500 years ago. What we find is that God created some fish and birds, but everything else came from what Genesis calls "the Earth". If God had created them, it would have said so, but he didn't. Evolution did some of it and the Titans started manufacturing what remained so that the animals would be the way they wanted them. ---- God was not too happy, by the way. If we follow on down, we find that on the 6th time period, man is REMADE to REPLENISH the earth [we can understand that the reason the repopulating was required was that everyone died [in a war].. What this means is that the Titans made these animals before the Heaven War that destroyed the Titans and the dinosaurs 65 million years ago. We will find out later that the DNA codes were saved for a number of the animals, so don't feel too sad.

*Genesis 1: 21- 28 So **God created the great sea creatures --, and every winged bird** -- And God said, "**Let the earth** bring forth -- livestock and creeping things and beasts ---- Then God said, "**Let us remake man in our image**, after our likeness. So God created man in his own image, -- God said unto them, Be fruitful, and multiply, and **replenish the earth**,*

Just because people were smart does not mean they made animals. I know that doesn't prove everything, but what if there was written proof to confirm the missing pieces? Many ancient texts tell us the same thing over and over. Ancient people created all types of animals including manipulation of ape-men to turn them into more "Man-like" beings. For those not knowing, our current success rate in this field is a cow that now has 16 percent human components. It won't be long before we can make our own dinosaurs. Anyway!!!!! Let's look at some of the major works of the past. The first stop is the Jewish Essene book of "Enoch". The book of Enoch is part of the Ethiopian Bible and mentioned in our current Bible as a great work, so let's see what the book had to say.

Enoch

*You [**the Anak people**] have been in heaven, but all the mysteries had not been revealed to you and you knew the worthless mysteries, and these in the hardness of your hearts you have made known to women and through these mysteries women and men work much evil on Earth—say to them therefore, "You have no peace.*

7:5-6 And the ANAK began to sin against birds, and beasts, and reptiles, and fish, and to devour one another's flesh, and drink the blood.

Identical to Biblical accounts and many other texts, Titans who eventually became the ANAK people sinned against animals. This does not mean that animals had sex with them, it simply means that the animals were genetically mutated. They became "unclean" as referenced throughout the Bible. Some would have been dinosaur like MONSTERS.

10:10-11-Restore the Earth, which the ANAK have corrupted; and announce life to it, that I may revive it. All the sons of men shall not perish in consequence of every secret, by which the Angels have destroyed, and which they have taught their offspring. All the Earth has been corrupted by the effects of the teachings of Azazyal

This Azazyal was one of the Anak people that began teaching "later" humans how to make animals.

ENOCH II

This is another Essene text.

31

59:5-6- But whosoever kills a beast without wounds, kills his own soul and defiles his flesh. And he who does any beast any injury whatsoever, in secret, it is evil practice, and he defiles his own soul.

The killing and injury done in secret was not killing animals for food, it wasn't torturing an animal either. Neither of those things would defile one's soul. It was, most likely, genetic manipulation and corruption by integrating man's genetic material. Imagine a half human dinosaur monsters.

Jubilees

Still another Essene Text [This one is also found in the Ethiopian Bible.]

*4:8- And lawlessness increased on the earth and **all flesh corrupted its way,** alike men and cattle and beasts and birds and everything that walks on the earth -all of them corrupted their ways and their orders, ---7:3- And after this [The war] they sinned against the beasts and birds.* There are two ways to sin against beasts- sex and genetic manipulation. God didn't like either. The corrupted animals were known as "unclean" monsters.

Jasher

Still another Essene Text. This one is also found in the Ethiopian Bible and referenced in our current Bible.

*4:18-19 and the sons of men in those days took from the cattle of the Earth, the beasts of the field and the fowls of the air, and **taught the mixture of animals of one species with the other**, in order therewith to provoke the Lord; and God saw the whole Earth and it was corrupt, for all flesh had corrupted its ways upon Earth, all men and all animals. And the Lord said, I will blot out man that I created from the face of the earth, yea from man to the birds of the air, together with cattle and beasts that are in the field for I repent that I made them.* Corrupted animals did not mean the animals were evil, it meant that the species were changed inappropriately. Most had become "unclean" or "abominable" monsters. The animals were to be destroyed because they had been "Modified".

Book of Naphtali

This is one on the Gnostic book found in the Nag Hammadi Desert of Egypt many years ago. The Gnostic Teachings tell us the same thing.

1:25-26- The Gentiles went astray, and forsook the Lord and changed their order, and obeyed stocks and stones, spirits of deceit—become not as Sodom, which changed the order of nature.

Not only does it indicate that the watchers or angels and gentiles [not pure Adamic humans that came after the Titans] practiced genetic manipulation, but also that the practice was the major cause for the flood.

Book of Creation

This is another Gnostic Version.

*Samael [Satan] said," I have no need for anyone-it is I who am God, and there is no other one that exists from me"---Pisitis [**God**] was filled with anger and said " You are mistaken, Samael, there is an immortal man of light that has been in existence before you, and who will appear **amid the creatures you have made,** and will trample you, and you will descend to the abyss--- then he and his followers made a great war in the seven heavens.* Like the Sumerian version, Satan and his cohorts designed animal monsters s to fight in the first Heaven War. Many of the monsters he designed were huge dinosaurs.

Generations of Adam

This is another Gnostic Version. *[6:1-5] Among our little ones was Timnor and Ammah. Timnor understood physical law and created mighty machines. Ammah understood the secrets of creation. She manipulated the very fountain of life until she had created new forms of beings dedicated to the destruction of mankind [8:4] Timnor and Ammah practiced every abomination. Tranter learned the ways of his mother Ammah and he did manipulate the very **nature of man and beast to create new forms which God had not ordained.** Another son Lukas traveled far* *abroad amongst the children of Adam, gathering knowledge to create a great center of learning.*

As in other texts, manipulation of species was common practice and the results were not always helpful to man and were always against God. Here we also find that the genetic breeding included changing men into something else and creating monsters.

"ZAND-AKASIH"

From ancient Persia we find this text that tells us the same thing.

Satan miscreated creatures and they became useless. God saw the defiled and bad creatures, they did not delight Him. Satan's was downfall was the unrighteous creation of the creatures and ignorance.

Satan and the soon to be rebels during the Heaven Wars defiled God's creatures with genetic manipulation. They became unclean monsters.

"Zadspram"

This is a ninth century translation of very ancient texts from the Zoroastrian faith. In this work Ahriman is Satan, but I think you can appreciate the descriptions of dinosaurs.

In the beginning of creation the whole Earth was delivered over into the guardianship of the sublime. After the great rain in the beginning of the creation—after the rain, was torn up by noise and wind. A portion, moreover, as much as one-half of the whole Earth, and each of six portions around. The middle one is Pars [moon] and the lofty mountains grew up on the north so that they might become separate one from another and imperceptible. Even before the coming of the destroyer, the creatures of antagonism came to the Earth??

Even before the heaven war, the Titan Monsters had been created.

And Ahriman [Satan] reported, "I will modify all types of life". They will be abominations to thee, God, and they will do my bidding."

This tells us a lot about these monsters. This Satan character planned the heaven war and decided to create monsters that God considered Unclean. These "seductions of material life" or dinosaurs were the same ones that the Sumerians identified as being created to allow Satan to win a war with those in Heaven.

And God said, "I will smite thee, Ahriman, and your creatures which thou thinkest have produced fame for thee. I will destroy everything about them as well." God warned Satan not to go against him and acknowledged that he had made a large quantity of monsters. Of course this is a reference to the genetic manipulation experiments to create the largest and meanest dinosaurs.

Time made the creatures of God move differently than the Ahriman's Creatures moved. Satan's creatures were substantially different than normal creatures. Satan's animals were known as abominations or "UNCLEAN". This would have included ALL Dinosaurs.

After the noxious creatures died, and the poison there form was mixed upon the Earth—The monsters that were created by the rebel angels to fight in the heaven wars almost all died in the wars. This happened at the end of the Cretaceous Period.

"The Story of Anus"

In this book, the Hittites had a somewhat funny version of the genetic manipulation in our ancient past. *During a plot to overthrow the Taru, Kumarbi lay with a Rock as if it were a woman. The rock bore a god that was solid rock, named Ullikummis. He was born to be used as a weapon to defeat the Taru. Initially, seventy gods attacked Kumarbi and he beat them. Taru fought with the Dragon Illuyankas and his children. A mortal named Hupasiyas helped in the dragon's destruction. Sharruma had a human head on a bull's body. Taru battled the Stone-god, Ullikummis, and finally defeated him after several battles. Kumarbi was defeated by Taru and Anus and later became 'the father of all gods'.*

This is referencing Titans or Anak people designing Monsters to help them take over heaven or it could have been just normal rock sex. I have no idea if the rock got any pleasure from the encounter. During the Heaven Wars, dragons were also created. Like the other dinosaurs and monsters, they also were defeated. It is interesting to note that the dragon is singled out as the most powerful monster in many histories. Another monster was made during the wars, sort of a backward Minatare. Battles against Heaven were finally won by the Heaven team, but it was not easy. Kumarbi and the others that followed him were, most likely, the ANAK who were finally kicked out of Heaven. They were kicked out of heaven only to become the rulers of Earth.

"Enuma Elish"

According to "The Epic of Creation (*Enuma Elish*)" and "Epic of Gilgamesh", the Sumerians tell about the same story as the Hittites. *The Igigi, under the direction of Taimat rebelled against Enlil, and surrounded heaven. --One of the gods, Hubur, created a horned serpent, a mushussu-dragon, a lahmu-hero, an ugallu-demon, a scorpion-man, umu-demons, a fish-man, a bull-man, and others to fight in the war.*

These Igigi genetically altered everything. Many monsters besides the Dragon were created especially for the heaven war. Certainly the dinosaurs were made. The bull-man was like the Minotaur from Greek Mythology and like the half bull half man of the Hittite history. I know this doesn't specifically say dinosaur, but you get the picture.

Taimat made the dragon to be as a god to fight in the war.

The dragon was not just another pretty face, but was so powerful, he was like a god. We will find this identical reference in the Jewish accounts. Later this monster would be known as the Leviathan.

"Epic of Gilgamesh"

This Babylonian Version sounds very familiar.

*She [Shamhat –[**one of the Titans**] must take off her clothes and reveal her attractions. Do for the primitive man, as women [**Titans**] do. She pulled not away, Enkidu was aroused. --- afterward- the gazelles saw Enkidu and scattered, for Enkidu had stripped--- his body was too clean [**the hair was all gone**]. His **legs were diminished**-he could not run as before, he had become wiser—Enkidu, you have become like a god.*

I assume the powerful Titans sort of forced themselves to sleep with this lowly creature. Their desire was to make a better servant. The hybrid mutation became intelligent.

"Book of Dzyan"

In Mongolia, the Book of Dzyan became their Bible. Here is what it says.

At the fourth level [of heaven], the sons were told to create their images. One third refused & two thirds obeyed. A curse was pronounced; they will be born on the fourth, suffer and cause suffering. This is the first war. There were battles fought between the Creators and the Destroyers, and battles fought for space; the seed appearing and re-appearing continuously. They slew the forms that were two- and four-faced. They fought the goat-men [Satyrs], and the dog-headed men, and the men with fishes' bodies.

This is not only describing the first heaven war, but also is discussing genetic breeding like that used to create the dinosaur monsters. Even the indication that 1/3 of the angels rebel is consistent with the Biblical version of this very ancient time in history. There have been many destruction periods on the earth. The seed re-appearing idea presented here seems to refer to re-establishment of animals after each successive destruction period by genetic replacement as I have presented earlier. The outcome of the breeding was sometimes not good. The men with fish bodies are of particular interest as the Sumerians, Dogon, and Hindu all worshiped such a creature. As I presented, these part human creatures were possibly considered monsters as well. In this case it would be referring to seraphim that sided with the rebel angels during the heaven wars.

Greek Mythology

I'm sure you recognize the Greek version.

*Gaia [Satan], after the defeat of her Giants, created [**genetically manipulated**] Typhon [half serpent/ half man] to take revenge on the gods.*

This may have been a reference to the creation of the Dragon for use in the Heaven War.]

Mongulala Tribe

The Mongulala tribe of Brazil was an ancient tribe that traced their ancestry back thousands of years. Let's see what they said about creating animals.

The gods taught us the secret of man, animals, and plants. The Blood Age was the beginning of the Mongulala history. It started immediately after the Golden Age. Critical information about the events of the era was written on animal skins.

According to this, **genetic manipulation to make monsters** was known prior to the flood. This Age of Blood was after the Golden Age. It seems to be talking about the huge number of wars before the flood. Evidently, this was the time when the world was governed by the Anak people.

"Popul Vuh"

The Popul Vuh was the holy book of the Maya. They also knew about the genetic manipulation of animals in very ancient times. Let's see if they had the same information.

Then "he" made more humans out of wood. Let us make him who will nourish and sustain us. We have tried with our first creations; but we could not make them praise and venerate us. So, then, let us try to make obedient, respectful beings. The creations looked like real people, but did not praise god because they had no memory, had no souls, and learned too much. An imposter named Vukub-Cakix and his giant sons challenged the Gods. God wreaked revenge by turning the world upside down.

38

This goes along with the probability that the Titans make hybrid monsters by genetic manipulation. This new human looked different than the earlier creatures. They were more like the Titans. The Titans taught this man too much about the worldly things. There is substantial concurrence here of an attempted overthrow of heaven. While our Bible simply indicates that the earth became void and without form, geologic history shows that the Earth axis flips frequently, just like this historical record indicated.

"Book of Secrets"

I saved the last 2 for now because they explain how mad God got at all the genetic manipulating and breeding and dinosaur monsters and the whole bit. The "Book of Secrets" found with the Dead Sea Scrolls provides a strong warning about the use of "secrets of God". The book simply says that if we use genetic manipulation and magic, the same thing will happen to mankind that had happened before. The earth would be destroyed again. This destruction would not be by direct intervention of God, but because we, as humans, don't understand what we are doing as we manipulate "Nature". Of the secret elements indicated in the text, it seems that the "manipulation of creation" or genetic manipulation is the worst. This seems to reference both genetic manipulation and transmutation of one material into another [Alchemy]. By all accounts, the Titans, later ANAK and humans continuously employed both of these things before and immediately after the flood. Here are the major elements of what has been pieced together of the "Book of Secrets". Judge for yourself. If it makes you fearful, you read it correctly.

Those who would penetrate the origins of knowledge, along with those who hold fast to the wonderful mysteries of magic and life.

This is talking about Titans, ANAK, and humans that practice the secrets of "life". The concept of penetrating the ORIGINS of knowledge lets us know that this is very ancient science being discussed in these verses so we can believe this was done during the time of the dinosaurs to create the beasts.

With this I beseech your attention. All of the secrets of sin magic, and **manipulating life** *were known but they [the ancient humans] did not know the secret of the way things are nor did they understand the things of old.*

This section indicates that no one knew the ramifications of meddling with nature before the flood. It is saying no one understood the REAL effects of using things like genetic mutation, creation of monsters, and Alchemy.

They did not know what would come upon them, so they did not rescue themselves without the secret of the way things are.

Magic did not warn or save ANAK, TITAN, or Cro-Magnon from the flood. This thing called the "SECRET OF THE WAY THINGS ARE" is a secret that was not known to anyone. The monsters created were abominations]

What shall we call man who will call no one on earth wise or righteous? It is not a human possession to act on wisdom. It is not possible because wisdom is hidden except for the wisdom of cunning evil, and the schemes of Belial who modified creation, a thing that ought never to be done again, except by the command of his Maker.

This is the important part. Only God has the wisdom to modify creation. Belial (a term for Satan) **modified creation** and it should NEVER be done again. This seems to include genetic manipulation, alchemy, and all the other magic areas.

You have not become wise in understanding my secrets of life and the earth; for you have not properly understood the origin of Wisdom.

Here is all one has to do to be able to correctly use "magic". In order to understand **how to manipulate nature in a good way**, you must understand how it came into being. Unfortunately, you cannot because you didn't exist when this Wisdom" was established.

"The Book of Giants"

Like the Book of Secrets, the Book of Giants confirms the art of genetic manipulation and the mess that occurs from it. The best way to describe what was in the "Book of Giants" is to present the portion that is still extant. You will see that God was certainly annoyed at the giants eating men, but according to this book and several other texts, the real kicker was the biological experimentation that the Giants did to the animals. We will never know the extent of their modification of species, but God hated it. Here is the "Book of Giants". To show how messed up the document is, a piece of the book is shown to the right. After each verse is a short interpretation. [They are my interpretations, so take them for what they are worth.]

*For they [**Titans,**] knew the secrets of heaven and sin was great in the Earth because of their experiments. They made mistakes and they killed many animals and people. They had sex with women and they begat giants.*

Like other groups of humans, these Titans and their offspring experimented with genetics and made monsters.

They selected two hundred donkeys, two hundred asses, two hundred rams of the flock, two hundred goats, two hundred other beasts of the field. The ANAK performed unnatural acts [on this group], and begat giants and dragons. From every animal, and from every type of human was taken its seed for mixed sex.

It strongly suggests that human and animal genes were mixed together to make nasty monsters.

After a time they defiled the animals and people and begot giants, monsters, and dragons. God saw all that they begot, and, behold, all the Earth was corrupted with their blood and by the hand of man. They were brought food which did not suffice for them and they turned on mankind. They began to get hungry and they were seeking to devour many animals and people. The people ran to a safe place but the monsters and dragons attacked it. Man's flesh was eaten by all the giants. monsters, and dragons. The monsters thought that they would be saved and they would arise after death, but it was not so because they were lacking in true knowledge of heaven and because they were abominations of the Earth.

If that wasn't bad enough, the giants started eating people. The giants and even the monsters did not understand that they would not go to a heavenly place after death and I'm sure their parents told them about the marvels of this other world.

They grew corrupt and did not worship the almighty God. They were considering separation of Giants]from the angels upon [the Earth, but to no avail. In the end they will perish and die because they caused great corruption in the Earth and because they tormented the Earth. Suffice to say they will be tormented after death.

The giants were doomed because they corrupted just about all animal life.

Titans Were Busy

Again and again the Titan people went to their stash of genetic components that made up animals and re-made the creatures like dinosaurs as they had done many time before. Some of the beasts were genetically manipulated to fight against the heavenly host. This was attested to by the Sumerian, Greeks, and the Jewish historians. God, of course, created the creatures initially, but the ancient people modified them relentlessly and sometimes with horrifying results. This genetic manipulation became commonplace. Even with some pretty amazing creatures being generated for the purpose of taking control of a place called heaven, the "Rebels" lost the war.

As you would expect, the losers were punished. They were modified to become the human beings [the ANAK people]. After the punishment, these guys continued making weird animals and taught later humans about the wonders of changing species.

Hopefully you can tell from these texts that genetic manipulation was rampant prior to the flood time and most likely after the flood it continued in a strong way. The most manipulation occurred during the Age of the Dinosaurs.

Experimental Modification

So we know that they were smart enough and the ancient texts try to indicate that genetic manipulation was accomplished during the very ancient times, is there additional evidence?. That question brings us to one of the most obvious statements about the vast number of inappropriate animal changes. GOD would not have "experimented" with size, characteristic, speed, eating methods and other items that did not foster an increase in civilization or survival. Some say that this obvious "experimenting" with animals proves that there is NO GOD.

Well, they are probably are right in thinking God wouldn't make mistakes, but still they are totally wrong.

God would not have done the experimenting, but the evidence suggests that the only reasonable conclusion for creation is that a single creator [God] must have initially designed the animals and all other life-forms.

God wouldn't do all this experimenting and Evolution would not allow it. Something else is most likely the answer.

Albertosaurus Mistake

In Canada an odd dinosaur was found. The odd thing that is noticed is that his hairdo. I don't even think there were Mohawk Indians back then, but there you have it the dinosaur tried to pretend he was one of them. And his beak was funny as well. That being said, the Albertosaurus also had the stupid tiny arms of the Tyrannosaurus. Mistakes were everywhere on this dinosaur, but somehow it survived. There can be little question that this animal grew in a lab not as an evolutionary process of survival of the fittest.

Nigersaurus Taqueti Mistake

This 110-million year-old dinosaur had a mouth like giant nail clippers, with hundreds of tiny teeth. The strange-looking Nigersaurus Taqueti shown to the right was discovered in the Sahara in 1997, however some of the bones from other similar animals were found back as early as the 1950s, so there were a fairly large number of these odd animals living at one time.. It was only 13 meters in length. It was a smaller cousin of the North American Diplodocus, but what it lacked in size it gained in teeth. Talk about weird looking, his jaw was flat, over half a meter long, and lined with more than 50 columns of teeth, adding up to over 500 teeth in total. If that wasn't weird enough, even with all the teeth, the skull weight was light because the bones were so thin, they were translucent. This was guy had a delicate head. Besides the huge almost transparent head and those impossible teeth, this African sauropod was different from a American diplodocus in a couple of other significant ways. Scientists checked the balance canal area of the brain and found out that, unlike most dinosaurs that carried their heads looking straight ahead, this one almost always had his massive head looking downward. I guess even with thin bones, having 500 teeth makes your head heavy on the end of a diplodocus like neck. Anyway, the other thing that is odd is that the entire backbone had the same almost transparent lightweight structure presumably to reduce its massive weight. This creature was not made to survive, but somehow it did for a while. This is another experiment gone wrong.

Raptorex Mistake

Some try to claim that the huge Tyrannosaurus Rex massive head and tiny, tiny arms was an act of evolution, but we know that it was an act of stupidity. Scientists are now beginning to agree with me on this after finding the Rapterex. This 9ft dinosaur, is almost identical to the carnivorous king with its puny forearms and athletic hind legs. but the Raptorex, which predates the T-rex by 60 million years, is also 100 times lighter. His arms weren't shortened to insure his weight could support the massive head, the arms were designed to be short or they were simply another mistake. They were not a mistake in nature, they were simply designed improperly. [left]

Mononykus Mistake

Potentially, the Rapterex experiment was funny enough to consider a second experiment and Monykus was born. Mononykus Olecranus *is a* rather strange dinosaur that has perplexed scientists and resisted a definitive classification. Like Raptorex, Mononykus's most distinctive feature is a pair of short, stunted forelimbs. To make him more silly, each of hands had only one functional finger and claw. The strange physiology of these short limbs has given rise to several competing hypotheses about the ancient animal's behavior. The small limbs' orientation may have made them useless for snatching prey or digging burrows but they may have survived by digging into nests of insects or simply pulled apart plants for digestion. Like the Tyrannosaurus, its running must have been scary as it could not use its arms for balance and probably fell over frequently. I'm sure this mistake was interesting to watch and laugh at. [previous right]

Pachycephalasaurus Mistake

The Pachycephalasarus was another genetically engineered thing. His head was so massive, that he probably had an extremely hard time lifting the thing. Almost solid bone, it was determined that his defense was to ram things. The head butt was his super power so to speak. What he lacked in ability due to his overly massive skull, he made up for in beauty, but there can be little discussion about this guy being another genetically generated mistake. His name is kind of neat, but he probably had headaches most of the time. [Next set left]

Spinosaurus Mistake

Let's look at the spinasaurus. His beak was so thin it was almost comical and his backbone brought back the fins of the Dimetrodon. His head and teeth were more like scissors than something workable. I'm sure many times he would attempt grabbing an animal only to chop it in half for others that probably stayed by his side to snatch his mistakes. The geneticists had to go back to the drawing board to modify this one. [Next set middle]

Velociraptor Mistake

Let me reintroduce you to the Velociraptor. Unlike the massive eating and hunting machines depicted in recent movies, it is believed that these birdlike animals carried wings with them. Certainly the wings were useless, but it would have made them silly looking. There is no doubt that their massive claws allowed them to be good hunters, but the wings still should be considered mistakes. [Next set right]

Long Nose Mistake

Sometimes "evolved features" are recognizable as mistakes. A Dinosaur mistake to be considered would be the long nosed

Dinosaur. As shown in the following picture his nose is over four times as long as his head and was curled back on itself. It was completely useless and there is no evidence to suggest that other dino-features evolved from this mistake. The nose couldn't be used as a battering ram like the horn extensions of other animals. It was just a long nose. For those who would suggest that this is the father of the elephant with his useful nose/hand, it would be improbable that the thing would have evolved from this characteristic to the dangly one of today. Let me repeat this factor.. This type of mistake probably didn't come from an omnipotent creator, nor did it come from an evolutionary process. This was a genetic mistake that happened to procreate for a time.

PARASAUROLOPHUS
The Long Nosed Dinosaur

"Ancient Humans" practiced Genetic manipulation over and over again. Although that seems to be a rash statement, it only makes sense. Beside the "no mistakes by God argument, a couple of the other reasons are given below:

Tropeognathus Mistake

Speaking of wings, the tropeognathus comes to mind. The idea of a flying lizard is odd enough, but when you add the club at the end of the bill, you have to start laughing at this one. Don't go claiming a massive module at the front of the beak made it more aerodynamic. And made it easier to eat stuff. Both are utterly false. This guy was another mistake. [Next Left]

Sail Head Mistake

Skeletal restoration of Tapejara Wellnhoferi from the Early Cretaceous of Brazil with soft-tissue reconstruction of cranial crest and membranous wing in downwind sailing posture. With a tail rudder on its head and a spindly, bat-like body, Tapejara Wellnhoferi may appear fit for nothing but extinction. [Next Right]

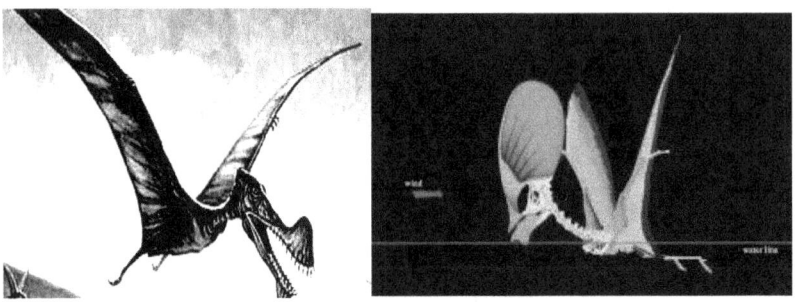

Animals Regenerated

After the various "extinction periods millions of years ago, animals quickly regenerated after major destruction periods on Earth. The animals regenerated much too quickly to have been the objects of haphazard and undirected evolution. This explosion of animals would have been impossible unless someone kept the genetic codes separate from the destruction and used them to re-introduce various species. It was genetic breeding that allowed them to revive so quickly. There aren't many other reasonable choices.

Dead Dinosaurs

During the time that the Ancient humans were in control, a massive list of strange and inappropriate animals rose that, like the bombardier beetle, don't fit the natural order. The genetic chain of events is more like "randomized limit experimentation", where strange and exotic breeds became more exotic and bizarre. Then these bizarre creatures were increased in size and, soon, the Earth was filled with Dinosaurs. They were the apparent rulers of the land. Giant dinosaurs roamed all around the world and died by the millions making all the precious oil that we find today. **Hurray for gigantic dead dinosaurs!!**

Dinosaur Extermination

Most of the dinosaurs that remained alive died abruptly at the end of the Cretaceous Period because a huge meteor which hit the

Yucatan, sprayed Iridium dust around the world, split open the continent of India, and caused huge volumes of magma to be expelled which choked out the life giving oxygen and light from the planet. There were other reasons for their demise like the earth slowing down and not being able to fly or even breath anymore, but the magma thing is more like what you were told in school. All of a sudden, the Age of the Titan Dinosaurs was over.

End of the Titan Monsters

While the development of the Beasts of the Titan Age is somewhat known, the Creationist viewpoint describes a time when there was perfection in design of the monsters that is not sustainable, and Evolutionist characterizes this as a time that was chaotic and unsustainable. Neither works as the Titans developed many of these monsters without regard for the animals themselves. They made them as a show of force. We'll look at some of the many mistakes "developed". While the development of the Titan Monster is sometimes laughable, the theories that were developed to describe why they all died is certainly laughable. Let's look at some.

Meteor Theory

This is by far the most discussed idea concerning the death of the dinosaurs. A huge meteor hit the earth and pushed dust around the world. This blocked the sun and BAM! Every BIG thing is dead. While it doesn't address the initial causes for the dinosaurs getting huge in the first place, it uses SOME physical evidence and expands it to build a somewhat absurd picture. The proof of this hypothesis lies in a layer of iridium dust particles called the K-T boundary that was deposited at the same time that the dinosaurs disappeared. This iridium stuff is fairly rare on earth, but very common in meteors so that is where the whole meteor strike idea comes from. I'll be talking about this episode later, because that part is well tested.

The hypothesis starts off with this huge meteor that hit the Yucatan at the end of the Cretaceous Period and spread the caustic dust everywhere. The dust supposedly choked out the light and life of our planet. All the monsters that had been around ceased to exist.

Scientists found the layer and deposits around the world and they found the remains of a huge meteorite crater. To make the event even more scary, on the other side of the world, they found something horrifying. They found that the earth actually split open when the meteor hit and huge amounts of magma were expelled onto the surface of the earth making most of what is now called India. Hundreds of cubic miles of magma spewed up for a long time after the Meteor hit. It was a scary time. The dinosaurs essentially disappeared around this same time so there is little doubt of some of the elements of the hypothesis. The problem is that a lot of this idea makes no sense at all. First of all, most of the dinosaur bones have been found UNDER the layer of iridium known as the K-T Layer so they died before the meteor struck. I suppose one could believe that the dinosaurs had an intuition about the impending doom and were frightened to death, by the dust. It would have been nice of them to die this noble way, but, in my opinion, we still cannot completely trust this absurd theory.

Assuming that many died AFTER the meteor struck, supposedly the dinosaur monsters were weaker than the tiny and insignificant rodents that survived. While today's rats probably would be good survivors, these initial creatures were not stronger, more powerful, more adaptable, more intelligent, or more evolved than the dinosaurs. The new creatures that sprang to life under mysterious circumstances should have died with or instead of the dinosaurs. Besides, while the dust may have caused a slight reduction in temperature which could have brought on famine, an equally logical theory says that the dust would have most likely covered the atmosphere such that the temperatures would have increased which could have allowed for vegetation to flourish. More vegetation would have been better for the dinosaurs. Good or bad the small mammals that would generally have been eaten by the larger monsters during this time. Small mammals should not have flourished as the monsters died. In general one can suppose that bigger is better not the other way around. Larger animals today live longer, control their environment better and usually eat the smaller creatures. In the old days the same general theme should have applied. I know you are going to say roaches would have survived, but the delicate mammals of that time were not roaches and dust did not kill the dinosaurs. We must investigate further.

Egg Theory

This is another popular one. In this hypothesis, tiny mammals killed all the dinosaurs by eating their eggs. The proof is in the large quantities of violated nests found during the same general time as the K-T boundary, but it is pretty much known that the only reptiles that survived during this time were the small ones and that causes a problem. If one is to consider this hypothesis he must first suppose that the other "smaller" reptile eggs were too small for the rodents to eat and that it was easier to fight off a weak, docile, and HUGE mother monstrous dinosaurs than fight off a ferocious, intimidating, horrifying, tiny insignificant mother lizard. Here is where we get even more strange. Some would contend that the huge monsters were too slow to fight off the mighty rats, but they would have died off much earlier as the gigantic, slow dinosaurs sort of stood around waiting for other gigantic, not quite as slow, dinosaurs to eat them. Others would contend that the mother monsters didn't have mothering instinct to protect the little ones, but the evidence shows a different story with mother monsters protecting their young just like modern alligators and crocodiles. Not too many rodents eat those luscious crocodilian eggs and crocodiles are still not extinct today. Mother monsters would have looked at many egg eating rodents as snacks. --- Egg eating didn't kill the dinosaurs! The mother monsters must have been dead from something else that happened and the eggs were left unguarded so the mammals could feast away.

Small Hearts Theory

This one starts off with part of an answer, but it goes terribly wrong. This one states that monster dinosaur hearts could not pump blood to their bodies efficiently and that caused their demise. The proof lies in the knowledge that the heart cavities were not large enough to support blood flow that could support running. Without running, it is said that the hunter dinosaurs could not hunt and soon they all died. While it's hard to disagree with the premise, if dinosaurs could never run, they would NEVER have survived in the first place. Just think about a short armed Tyrannosaurus trying to slowly reach his huge head down and get some other slow moving food. The picture seems almost comical. Some have stated that because the Tyrannosaurus arms were so short, any fast motion would place him in jeopardy of falling over. He could not protect his fall and even if his heart were big enough, his tiny arms would have eventually killed him. The great finds of this oddball monster tell us a different story. He was king during his heyday and it wasn't his heart that killed him. Let me tell you another thing. The Tyrannosaurus also ran or he would not have eaten. I know you have been told the Tyrannosaurus was like a vulture and waited for things to die before he would eat, but I tell you this is an impossible scenario. If he was too slow to kill a prey, he certainly would be too slow to get the prey after death because many other "fast" dinosaurs would have taken the food before he could get his meal. Some tell us the huge brachiosaurus was so huge that even being in the water much of the time to support his weight, blood flow was an impossible situation in its miles and miles of arteries and veins. While it was impossible for the brachiosaurus to survive, it survived very well for millions of years. It's heart didn't have trouble pushing oxygen to the different parts of the huge brachiosaurus body so it could stretch its head up to the tops of the trees for the best food stuff.

Plate Tectonics Theory

This is one is gaining acceptance, but I have no idea why. In this hypothesis the super continent Pangea began to separate. Its separation might have somehow killed the dinosaur monsters as plate tectonics rammed together crustal plates enough to push dirt almost 5 miles into the sky. While the split of Pangea has been theorized to have begun about the beginning of the Mesozoic Age, during the height of the dinosaur rule, it is surmised that major Himalayan Mountain plate smashing would have really messed up the environment and killed the fragile dinosaurs and left those mighty rats at the end of the Cretaceous. The whole plate movement thing is true, but the idea that plates smashed together and made mountains is absurd. Instead, the evidence seems to indicate that the 1st of the 2 major "world ring" mountain ranges, called the American ridge came into existence well before a terrible catastrophe at the end of the Permian Age. The evidence indicates that the planet Mars came very close to our planet and the gravitational attractions of the 2 planets pulled up massive sections of both planets along what had been the equatorial boundaries. The ridge runs perpendicular to the equator and along the western coastlines of both Americas and around the other side through portions of the Far East. You guessed it. 2nd of the 2 great mountain ranges, the Himalayan ridge, running generally in the direction of the present equator along the top of India and through China, came into existence when Pangea began to split because of the same thing. Mars again moved too close to our planet during another pass during the Triassic and it was far worse this time as both planets were even closer together. Mars was ripped in half and on earth the Pacific Ocean was formed as a huge chunk of our planet blasted away into space. I will have go over the development of these strange mountain ranges in more detail later as they have something to do with the development of the huge dinosaurs, but they were not the cause of their demise nor did plate tectonics have ANYTHING to do with their development. Get that out of your head!!!

Biblical Day Theory

I'm sure that many have heard this one as it is touted as the religious hypothesis. Some call it the creationist view. By this misinterpretation, the earth and everything that was made before the creation of Adam was made in only 6 days and dinosaurs never existed in the multiple millions needed to produce the vast oil reserves we have today. God sort of stuck the oil down there because he knew we would need it later. The proof is in the Hebrew word "Yowm" which can be interpreted as "day". One of the interpretations of the first chapter of "Genesis" is that the changes in the world that lead to the creation of a "6th day[yowm]" man were compressed into 5 days or 24 hour periods. Not only are there major problems with interpreting a Yowm as a 24 hour day in this great and important book, there is a strong indication that between the first and second verse, a major disturbance occurred to make the earth become "without form and void". Besides those 2 elements, other problems include the requirement for God to rest on the 7th day because he was tired and the idea that God could only do so much creating each day. In order to get you to break away from others interpretations rather than reading the words, I'll go over this first section of our Bible in some detail. Don't get mad at me as I try to help you read the first chapter of "Genesis" again . Many times the dogmatic elements of religion have nothing to do with the Biblical teachings. We need to study the actual Biblical words and not ignore the information when trying to reconstruct the history of the dinosaur. What we find is that Moses' "Genesis" story and science completely agree.

Experimentation Theory

Following the more accepted Creationist view comes another with a little twist. In this one the creator was simply experimenting with different forms of animals and got tired of the dinosaur monster mold. The proof is in the thousands of different animal types that were generated and how many survived even though they were not the most practically designed creatures. In this extinction answer, dinosaur monsters and ALL huge animals vanished at the same time as if the creator lost interest in that experiment. While the strangeness of the oddball animal species is well known and the fact that less adapted creatures survived while more advanced ones disappeared through time, the idea that the creator experimented to get what he wanted seems absurd.

I will examine a number of the oddball shouldn't have survived monsters and characteristics, but we cannot stop there. One cannot believe that a creator God that can see everything would have need or desire to create misshapen and less than appropriate monsters. I suppose this hypothesis would say that the reason that huge monster dinosaurs are not here today is not that they could not survive here, but rather that God simply didn't want them to be here. Instead God wanted horrible viruses and smaller versions of dangerous animals to be let loose on the earth. God would also be responsible for people sometimes being born with two heads or as idiots, or with no arms—etc. etc. etc. Let's get off this kick about God messing up his controlled, physically perfect universe with magic tricks and go on to another idea.

Creative Design Theory

This hypothesis is really a corollary to the preceding idea. In it the creator may have made dinosaurs as a calculated evolution-like process to build towards his final creation of man. The proof of this discussion has been shown in the neatly drawn out evolutionary changes that SUPPOSEDLY happened over a neatly determined timeline. Tiny creatures evolved to larger ones to larger ones and then to larger ones. The problem is that this neat timeline is a lie. There is no logical progression of animal adaptations to the environment nor is there any logical reasons I can come up with concerning why God would do this evolution thing for a while and essentially have almost nothing happen since the flood. Think about it. Massive changes that "helped" evolution supposedly occurred over a very short time and then no change occurred for millions of years followed by another round of massive changes over and over again. Now let's look "After the Flood". I know some have indicated that red men, white men, black men, yellow men and olive skinned men all evolved from the original Noah clan immediately following the flood and never changed again after that fateful time, but the physical evidence and common sense tells a different story. By the way, changing of those minor characteristics isn't evolution in the first place. There have been NO recent species changes at all so the whole concept is flawed not only in common sense but also in its possibility of test.

Evolution Theory

That brings us another common one that is very similar to the preceding one. It can be called the uncontrolled, survival of the fittest, Darwinian evolution misconception. In it dinosaurs disappeared simply as a result of the actions of this evolution process and mammals were MORE EVOLVED than monster dinosaurs and therefore dinosaur doom was a foregone conclusion. The hypothesis is neat and tidy no successful components of it have been shown to contain any level of realism. Shells, for instance became more and more evolved, but reverted to our identical versions of today that cannot be distinguished from the extremely ancient versions. How could the first and lowest evolutionary models somehow become the most evolved models of various creatures. Many monster "evolutions" follow the same confusing back and forth, survival of the most unfit, or most obscure species versions as we look though time. Besides that there are way too many ANOMALIES that have to be contended with for this whole "evolution thing". Let's look at some of them before we go on.

Too many animal types- were spontaneously generated if an "evolution theory" was to be supported. Later we will see that after each destruction period, a huge influx of animals was apparently created within an extremely short period rather than the supposed "start over" that evolution theories would require. Each of the seven generally known major destructions recorded in history caused the extermination of well over 80% of all species of life and each time more animals emerged. Here is the strange part. The evolutionary life cycle didn't start over each time, but instead, many creatures spontaneously reappeared. To make things even stranger, a complete extinction record shows as many as 18 major extinction periods and many periods of minor extinctions during Earth's life cycle, which further exacerbates the problem. Quick regeneration of widely diverse life after extinction doesn't go along with evolution.

Out of Place Objects-Many things are out of place in time by evolutionary standards. Man's footprints in the same substrate as dinosaurs, manmade cups found imbedded coal, manmade walls found deep in the Earth, and many other artifacts clearly show that humans were on the Earth many years before the time that evolution can support. A sampling of these anomalies can be seen in later chapters. Don't be fooled into thinking that the artifacts are proof that the world is very young and testing methods are a sham. As I mentioned earlier, we will investigate some of the methods and reasons why a young Earth associated with the "creationist hypothesis" is not a better answer than the "evolution hypothesis", but it is no worse either. Both have to throw away too many pieces of evidence because they don't fit either mold.

Earth Shift Theory

If you don't already know, what you will find out later is that the earth rotational axis is not constant but instead wanders or jerks to new locations periodically and so it was at the end of the Cretaceous Period. This hypothesis centers around the same occurrence that quick-froze mammoths in Alaska and Siberia a mere 10 to 12 thousand years ago during the Pleistocene Extinction. The Earth's axis of rotation jumped and the rest is frozen in time. Areas that had been warm, froze solid and all the animals of that region were frozen as well. We find the evidence of this everywhere and therefore some believe that a similar "axis jerk" occurred during the Cretaceous Extinction and dinosaur doom was initiated. Dinosaur monsters would have been eating in a pleasant field one minute and the next they would be positioned in the Arctic and quickly they would be frozen. The problem is that some areas would have quickly frozen while others would have remained constant or would have become a "Nicer" climate. Some dinosaur monsters would have died off, but the species would have survived unless the entire species only was found in a small localized area. The evidence indicates that almost ALL huge dinosaurs became extinct at the same relative time 65 million years ago. I'm sure that some of the minor extinction times could be attributed to the earth's axis of rotation shifting, but to cause, essentially ALL dinosaur monsters to disappear is an impossible situation. [Later we will see that a few did survive.]

Genetic Manipulation Theory

His one is somewhat similar to some of the previous one except, in this hypothesis, man [called Titans by the Greeks] was on earth during the time of the dinosaur monsters. In fact, man had been on the earth and was completely civilized by the time of these monsters. A further extension of the seemingly bizarre set of parameters adds the probability that the reason that there were so many oddball types of creatures during the beginnings of our earth that man modified most of God's created animals for his own purposes. As we follow this thought, the creator was not responsible for the design of dinosaur monsters. Ancient texts classified the animals that were not made by the creator as "unclean" or "abominable". The creator simply got rid of the animals he didn't like. The proof of this discussion is in the fact that many dinosaurs and other animals show extremely inappropriate characteristics which a God would not have established and a survival of the fittest evolutionary process would not have allowed. A major problem with this hypothesis is that the whole concept of intelligent humans being on the earth millions of years ago is foreign to most of us and the assumption that God would not simply erase things he didn't like seems counter to our basic religious teachings. Many of the things we enjoy today would never have survived if that was our creator's method of dealing with us. The erasing would not conform to God's physical laws like those that define our physics and mathematics, assuming that "God is not the author of confusion" as is indicated in our most holy books.

Germ Theory

Here is another that has had some followers recently. In this hypothesis some type of germ infected dinosaur monster DNA which resulted in their extinction. The proof lies in the extinction of animals today as many species become extinct from viral infestation rather than environmental elements. Scientists know that major modification in DNA can be attributed to structural changes that result from the intrusion of a foreign agent into a chromosomal boundary. There is also the genetic mutations that occur from radiation intrusion as a result of a nuclear explosion. To add fire to this idea, there is a group that is investigating the almost instantaneous change in the human population some 6 thousand years ago. Apparently, around the world, humans and possibly other animals changed. They became much more primitive in capability, action, and civilization after some horrific event at that time. Whatever it was affected EVERONE by all accounts. To show how similarly this event is addressed, the culprit being investigated is some type of microbe that modified the DNA structure. I suppose it could have just as easily made man become extinct or dinosaurs. While it might have possibilities concerning extinction, it cannot explain why there are almost no huge animals today or why they got large in the first place, so we must continue or accept that huge monsters are still around.

Flatulence Theory

Don't laugh at this one, because some people have been afraid of high levels of flatulence for some time now and the fear is spilling onto the dinosaurs. Just like the fear of cattle, in this hypothesis monster dinosaur flatulence caused enough greenhouse gas in the atmosphere to disrupt environmental order which killed the dinosaurs and left only the Mammals. The proof lies in the amount of dinosaur remains [fossil fuels] and the huge amount of cattle flatulence that have been registered and focused on concerning greenhouse gas build up. In addition to the cattle there is the dozens of greenhouse theories concerning how the planet Venus met its untimely end. No, I'm not suggesting that cows were on Venus, but if cows make a difference today, dinosaurs passing gas would have almost ignited the place. This concept may make a little more sense as we investigate more about the Titan Monsters. The nitrates produced would not have destroyed plant-life. In fact, a slight increase in the atmosphere would have been good for the plant-life. By the way, greenhouse gasses building up on Venus by themselves could not have caused the calamity that occurred on that unfortunate planet and the evidence suggests that the inferno began a mere 12 thousand years ago, but that is another story. Let's leave this hypothesis with a question. Was anyone offended by the dinosaurs? Even if someone wanted to yell at them they probably didn't.

Man Kill Theory

As I mentioned before, the physical evidence and many, many ancient texts including our Bible, confirms an extremely ancient, civilized, human existence. Later we will look at many pieces of physical and written evidence that cannot easily be ignored concerning this matter. That being said, some are trying to pin the demise of the dinosaurs on this ancient group. In this hypothesis the ancient [Titan] humans that lived with the dinosaur monsters killed them off because they were too dangerous. The proof is provided in stone. Hundreds of pieces of evidence shows the civilized humans lived before the extinction and it would be reasonable to assume that they would want to eliminate the dinosaurs as a threat to their lifestyle and life. Possibly there were fears of the dinosaurs taking all the vegetation. Possibly the dinosaur flatulence discussed earlier was becoming a problem. Possibly the ancient man accidentally killed them with some type of DDT or similar substance. The concept of brain over brawn has always been an interesting story and concept. While there are many problems with this supposition, at least, it doesn't require ravenous and powerful rats to destroy the monsters and, unfortunately and it again doesn't explain why they got so big and why there are NO large land animals today. Besides you would think that they would have kept a few for their zoos and entertainment.

War Theory

This one seems out there as well, but it also has some insight that we can use. In this hypothesis there was a huge war between inhabitants of heaven and earth and the results of the war led to the almost complete extinction of everything including dinosaur monsters. If you remember, our Bible discusses such a war. This can be amplified by the fact that the second verse of the "Genesis" story seems to describe the aftermath of such a war that happened way before the creation of Adam. The odd part is that the Biblical book of "Jeremiah" indicates that many ancient cities were destroyed in the war that left the earth without form and void. If there were cities, there had to be people on earth before this very ancient war. All of this sounds very confusing, but we may come back to this very ancient war as we investigate further.

Dead Dinosaurs

During the time that the Ancient humans were in control, a massive list of strange and inappropriate animals rose that, like the bombardier beetle, don't fit the natural order. The genetic chain of events is more like "randomized limit experimentation", where strange and exotic breeds became more exotic and bizarre. Then these bizarre creatures were increased in size and, soon, the Earth was filled with Dinosaurs. They were the apparent rulers of the land. Giant dinosaurs roamed all around the world and died by the millions making all the precious oil that we find today. Hurray for gigantic dead dinosaurs!!

Dinosaur Extermination

Most of those that remained alive died abruptly when that huge meteor which hit the Yucatan, sprayed Iridium dust around the world, split open the continent of India, and caused huge volumes of magma to be expelled which choked out the life giving oxygen and light from the planet. There were other things going on as I explained earlier, but some of the animals miraculously survived and, of course, the ancient humans survived. Evidently, the dinosaur experiment was halted after this event, because they were not brought back. They were just too big and that "Tyrannosaurus Rex" design, with the stupid little arms was a real mistake. Later we will find that some smaller dinosaurs were re-engineered or survived various destructions, including the destruction associated with the worldwide flood described in the Biblical history. The earth could no longer support the really massive land giants, but evidence shows there were reduced size masters here as late as 3 thousand years ago. Two of these animals are listed in Jewish histories. These were the Leviathan and Behemoth. Here are a few of the texts that describe these monsters.

- ***II Esdras 6:48-***Then he set apart two creatures the Behemoth and the Leviathan. You put them in separate places. The country of 1000 hills was given to behemoth. To leviathan you gave the 7th part, the water *[**A few dinosaurs and sea serpents survived.***]*

- ***Job 40: 15-24-***Behold now **behemoth,** which I made with thee; he eateth grass as an ox. His strength is in his loins, and his force is in the navel of his belly. He moveth his tail like a cedar **[There are no cedar tailed hippos, but the huge Diplodocus dinosaur had a tail worthy of mentioning]**: The sinews of his stones are wrapped together. His bones are as strong pieces of brass; his bones are like bars of iron. He is the chief of the ways of God: He lieth under the shady trees, in the cover of the reed, and ferns. Behold, he drinketh up a river, and hasteth not: He taketh it with his eyes: his nose pierceth through snares.

- ***Job 41:1-***Canst thou draw out **leviathan** with a hook? Wilt thou play with him as with a bird? Or wilt thou bind him for thy maidens? Behold, the hope of him is in vain: shall not one be cast down even at the sight of him? None is so fierce that dare stir him up: His teeth are terrible round about. His scales are his pride, shut up together as with a close seal. One is so near to another that no air can come between them. They are joined one to another, they stick together, that they cannot be sundered. --His eyes are like the eyelids of the morning. Out of his mouth go burning lamps, and sparks of fire leap out. Out of his nostrils goeth smoke, as out of a seething pot or caldron. His breath kindleth coals, and a flame goeth out of his mouth. *[**This is a "Fire breathing Dinosaur"; possibly a reversed bombardier beetle.***]* The flakes of his flesh are joined together: When he raiseth up himself. The sword of him that layeth at him cannot hold: the spear, the dart, nor the habergeon. He maketh the deep to boil like a pot: he maketh the sea like a pot of ointment. He maketh a path to shine after him; one would think the deep to be hoary. Upon Earth there is not his like, who is made without fear. He beholdeth all high things: he is a king over all the children of pride. **[We're going to have some**

more discussions about dragons later, and find that they were "kings over the proud".]

Chromosomes

As creatures evolve, increasing the genetic information contained in chromosomes enhances species. This would be easily seen as an increase in chromosome packets; or so it would seem if there were anything to evolution enhancement or uncontrolled evolution in general. Below is a short list of common animal types. Beside each animal type is the number of chromosomes used as the building instructions. Notice that "Man" is much more highly evolved than most of the animals as it has more instructions. Wow! The theory works. Man is better than other animals because it is more highly evolved.

Virus	1	Ant	2
Parasitic roundworm	2	Indian deer	6
Fruit fly	8	Mustard	10
Microscopic roundworm	12	Rye	14
Guinea Pig	16	Dove	16
Corn	20	Horsetail plant	21
Opossum	22	Kidney bean	22
Redwood tree	22	Chinese deer	23
Earthworm	32	Yeast	32
Frog	36	Pig	40
Mouse	40	Wheat	42
Bat	44	**Man**	**46**
Tobacco	48	Apes	47
Sheep	54	Domestic Horse	64
Wild Horse	66	Dog	78
Chicken	78	Carp	104
Crayfish	200	Fern	500
Butterfly	380		

Ape Chromosome Count-Oh! No! It seems that we have de-evolved from the Apes by this logic. Apes, however, have one more pair of chromosomes because two sets of pairs; those called

64

2p and 2q, are put together in the human set as one chromosome pair, so the theory still holds as our DNA information is actually more compact in humans than in apes.

Backward DNA and Haplotyping-It should be noted here that almost all of the chromosomes are identical when comparing human and ape sets, so we possibly evolved from them. The only chromosome packets that differ are the 4th and 17th set. These two also are almost identical, but appear to be inverted such that the sequencing is the same but split in the middle and recombined in reverse order. So an ape is simply an "accidentally backward human" or the reverse with a man being an "accidentally backward Ape". No one knew which came first; the man or the Ape, but evolution is still supreme.

Later, DNA mutation experts [Haplotype scientists] told us the Chimpanzee and Bonobo apes definitely have fewer mutations so they came after humans and, mostly likely after Cro Magnon. This sounded strange, but later we will see how easy this would have been.

Butterfly Masters-Now we continue down the list and find we will have to continue evolving for some time to get up to the complexity of a dog, carp, or butterfly. We should either respect our master butterflies or disregard this crazy notion of advancement by evolution. Those flying insects know that they are better than us; we don't have to acknowledge it to make it true. Chromosomes acknowledge it for us.

Evolution isn't the Answer-I'm pretty sure you can see that the whole non-directed evolution theory has holes . A better theory is that animal were created and miscreated over and over again by well-meaning and sometimes vicious genetics specialists. I know we think of ancient people being Stone Age grunting dumb-dumbs, but that simply was not the case. Before a horrible war that occurred 6 thousand years ago, mankind civilizations were at a much higher level of development than we have today and the science of that time was better than the science of today. They DID make monsters.

Remade Monsters

The Bible tells us that the monsters created for the Heaven War were not completely annihilated. The ANAK made a huge quantity of unclean or abominable animals after the Heaven Wars had ended and many normal people were taught how to do the same thing and make even more bizarre animals from God's creations. Some of the better known ones were the Leviathan, Behemoth, and Dragon. Some of these animals actually made it past the great flood of Noah and the book of Daniel tells about how a dragon was worshipped until Daniel killed it to show it was not a god. Below are just a few of the many sources that tell us that monsters were remade after the Heaven War and were here up until the relatively recent past.

*Isaiah 27:1 -In that day the Lord with his hard and great and strong sword will punish **Leviathan** the fleeing serpent, Leviathan the twisting serpent, and he will slay **the dragon** that is in the sea.*

*Job 41:1-34 -"Can you draw out **Leviathan** with a fishhook or press down his tongue with a cord? Can you put a rope in his nose or pierce his jaw with a hook? Will he make many pleas to you? Will he speak to you soft words? Will he make a covenant with you to take him for your servant forever? Will you play with him as with a bird, or will you put him on a leash for your girls? ... Behind him he leaves a shining wake; one would think the deep to be white-haired.*

*Job 40-41-"Behold, **Behemoth,** which I made as I made you; he eats grass like an ox. Behold, his strength in his loins, and his power in the muscles of his belly. He makes his tail stiff like a cedar; the sinews of his thighs are knit together. His bones are tubes of bronze, his limbs like bars of iron. "He is the first of the* *works of God; let him who made him bring near his sword! ... -No one is so fierce that he dares to stir him up. Who then is he who can stand before me? Who has first given to me, that I should repay him? Whatever is under the whole heaven is mine. "I will not keep silence concerning his limbs, or his mighty strength, or his goodly frame. Who can strip off his outer garment? Who would come near him with a bridle? Who can open the doors of his face? Around his teeth is terror. ...*

Macedonian Account-*Just to let you know Daniel was not the only dragon killer, Alexander the Great even found and killed one of these miscreated beasts by feeding it poison and tar almost like his predecessor.*

Book of Abraham 4:24- *The gods prepared the Earth to bring forth the living things.- and the gods organized **the Earth** to bring forth the beasts.* **[This was not talking about the first creatrion of animals, but the second creation after the Heaven Wars by the Anak humans that were referred to as gods by the "normal people"]**

II Esdras 6:48- *On the 6ᵗʰ day you ordered **the Earth** to produce for you cattle, wild beasts, and creeping things.* **[Certainly God did not create them, the earth created most of the animals as was commonly known to the ancient Jewish writers. This is talking about the second creation of abominable animals by the ANAK.]**

AMOS Description- In Amos 9:3 it speaks of *"a serpent to bite the people who try to hide in the sea from God"*. The one pictured might very well have been something like the one Amos warned against.

Daniels Account

If Dragons were real, how would you get rid of them? A special weapon is described in one of the books of the Bible. Unfortunately the chapter discussing the way to kill dragons was removed from edited versions of the Bible made after 1826, but the original canon of the "Vulgate Bible" certainly contained the information. The removed section was the last chapter of the Book of Daniel. This chapter of Daniel, sometimes called "Bel and the Dragon", tells of a weapon made by Daniel to defeat a dragon that had survived the flood and the Tower of Babel War. Not only does this discuss a great weapon, but also it gives us additional confirmation of Dragons surviving the flood. There was a problem concerning reintroduction of Dragons. Once they were made, the people had an extremely difficult time feeding the monsters. The feeding thing included sacrificing virgins so I'm not getting into that part of monsters in this book. It is simply too scary.

Daniel 23:28-*"And in that same place there was a great dragon, which they of Babylon worshipped. He liveth, he eateth and drinketh; thou canst not say that he is no living god: therefore worship him. Daniel said give me leave, O king, and I shall slay this dragon without sword or staff. Daniel took pitch, and fat, and hair, and did seethe them together, and made lumps thereof: this he put in the dragon's mouth, and so the dragon burst in sunder:*

Not only does this verse from the book of Daniel show that Dragons were alive after the flood, but it also indicates that Daniel was able to make some kind of bomb. Maybe making a dragon explode wasn't difficult if they breathed fire already, but let's credit Daniel just the same. You might wonder why this particular verse of Daniel was removed while allowing the remaining portion to be part of our most holy book. The thing that upset people about this verse is not that they thought the book of Daniel was a lie, but the fact that they [the caretakers of what people should read] could not come up with a way to put a dragon on Noah's Arc and there was consensus that all animals were on the arc. I think that all three are correct. The book of "Daniel" is telling the truth; dragons were not on the arc; and all animals were on the arc. Animals that were generated after the flood were not on the arc. One was called the Behemoth.

Gnostics Monsters

The Gnostic Jews had a slightly different understanding of the monsters of the day and those they were told about from long ago. They tried to understand about this mess and this is what they wrote in **"Generations of Adam".** The Story tells us about Adam's children. One thing the children did was to make animals and monsters.

[6:1-5] Among our little ones was Timnor and Ammah. Timnor understood physical law and created mighty machines. Ammah understood the secrets of creation. She manipulated the very fountain of life until she had created new forms of beings dedicated to the destruction of mankind. As in other texts, manipulation of species was common practice and the results were not always helpful to man and were always against God.

[8:4] Timnor and Ammah practiced every abomination. Tranter learned the ways of his mother Ammah and he did manipulate the very **nature of man and beast** *to create new forms which God had not ordained. Another son Lukas traveled far abroad amongst the children of Adam, gathering knowledge to create a great center of learning.*

The **"Cave of Treasures"** of the Gnostics also provides us some insight about this whole making animals and monsters thing. *And on the Fifth Day God commanded the waters, and they brought forth all kind of fish of divers appearances, and creatures which move about, and serpents, and Leviathan, and beasts of terrible aspects,*--This certainly indicates that there were creatures more terrible than the Leviathan.

Other Monsters

The Sumerians, Babylonians, Zoroastrians, Egyptians and the people of Nepal give us more insight. Some of their history of these monsters sounds identical, but some sounds bizarre.

The Sumerian Story

According to "The Epic of Creation (*Enuma Elish*)" and "Epic of Gilgamesh", the Sumerians tell about the manufacture of these animals.

The first children of the gods were the Lahmu - 'the hairy ones'. **[This is talking about genetically produced monsters.]** *The Igigi, under the direction of Taimat rebelled against Enlil, and surrounded heaven.* **[This is the heaven war discussed previously with Taimat taking the Satan position.]** *One of the gods, Hubur, created a horned serpent, a mushussu-dragon, a lahmu-hero, an ugallu-demon, a scorpion-man, umu-demons, a fish-man, a bull-man, and others to fight in the war.* **[Everyone said the same thing. Many monsters besides the Dragon were created especially for the heaven war. The bull-man was like the Minotaur from Greek Mythology and like the half bull half man of the Hittite history.]** *Taimat made the dragon to be as a god to fight in the war.* **[The dragon was not just another pretty face, but was so powerful, he was like a god. We will find this identical reference in the Jewish accounts.]**

The Babylonian Story

The Sumerians became the Babylonians. Babylonian version of the same story is called "Epic of Creation". It was written about 1200 BC, and it tells the same story again. My comments are in bold after each significant stanza. Again monsters of many types were mis-created.

*Taimat [same Taimat as the Sumerian history] said, "We will make monsters, and monsters and gods against gods will march into battle together." **[Like almost all the ancient texts, the leader of the rebellion began making beings to battle heaven.]** [She made]-snarling dragons wearing their glory like gods. **[Of all the monsters, the Dragon was made above the rest and given the "Glory of the gods" which other texts simply call the "light".]**-- He put in chains the eleven monsters, and all their murderous armament. **[Some of the beings and monsters were placed in chains just like the Jewish account.]***

Zoroastrian Beginnings

According to the "ZAND-AKASIH", part of the Zoroastrian Biblical Texts, we find a similar "monster creation story.

*During the fifth time, God created a cow and from it, he created 282 species of animals. Satan miscreated beings and they became useless. God saw the defiled and bad beings, they did not delight Him. Satan's was downfall was the unrighteous creation of the beings and ignorance. **[Satan and the soon to be rebel angels defiled God's beings with genetic manipulation.]**Satan also miscreated Akoman, and the other Demons. God saw that his creation was mixed with light and darkness.* [Satan made special monsters. They were made to fight in the heaven wars. The beings including humans and animals were becoming hybrids and abominations.]

Nepal Story

The *"Book of Dzyan"* is a collection of 9 Sanskrit tablets from Nepal. In them we find the descriptions of a total of 7 individual creations of humans over the years. Some of them were human, some were more spirit than human, but the information does go along with other data being presented.

*There were battles fought between the Creators and the Destroyers, and battles fought for space; the seed appearing and re-appearing continuously. **[There have been many destruction periods on the earth. The seed re-appearing idea presented here seems to refer to re-establishment of animals after each*** *successive destruction period by genetic replacement as I have presented earlier.]They slew the forms that were two- and four-faced. They fought the goatmen [Satyrs], and the dog-headed men, and the men with fishes' bodies.* **[The outcome of the breeding and genetic manipulation was sometimes not good. The men with fish bodies are of particular interest as the Sumerians, Dogon, and Hindu all worshiped such a being. In this case the creatures were made before the heaven wars.]**

Events after the Heaven War

We will be discussing the remaining races in the following books, but the book of Dzyan may give us some insights into what may be following.

*The **Fourth Race** finally developed speech. The fourth brown, which became black with sin. They became tall with pride. We are the kings, it was said; we are the gods. **They took wives** fair to look upon. Wives from the mindless, the narrow-headed. They bred monsters. Wicked demons, male and female.* **[The 4th creation was the ANAK. Just like the history provided in the book of Enoch, and the Bible, these beings took human wives. This indicates that the offspring were monsters, but we can tell from other works that genetic manipulation was also used to produce the monstrous creatures.][Fifth Race]** *Monsters they bred. A race of crooked red-hair-covered monsters going on all fours. A dumb race to keep the shame untold.* **[The "Book of Giants" indicated that there were giants and MONSTERS aftrer the war.]**

Egyptian Story

The "Egyptian Book of the Dead" shows similarities with the Bible and other ancient historical works in reference to some of the topics we have been studying. Here are some similarities.

Thine enemy the Serpent hath been given over to the fire. [Ra, took the form of a cat, and slew Apep, the prince of darkness, who had taken the form of a monster serpent The Serpent- fiend Sebau hath fallen headlong, his forelegs are bound in chains, and his hind legs hath Ra carried away from him. **[Like Biblical texts, the** *serpent monsters originally had arms and legs. Satan used them in his Heaven War.]The gods [The losers of the war who became rulers in the Earth] rejoice when they see Ra; his beams flood the world with light. Het-Henen-su, under the form of a horned, ram-headed man [**The depictions of monsters   are everywhere.]**Ra rose for the first time when the heavens and the earth were created as soon as Ra rose he separated the earth from the sky. Shu played at the Creation, when he held up with his arms and hands the sky which Ra had made to separate it from the earth. [Like many other histories, the Earth was split apart to become the earth and the sky or heavens.]Her-shef was a solar god he had four heads; one is the head of a bull, one that of a ram, and two are the heads of hawks. Above these are the characteristic horns of Khenmu Goddess Neheb-Kau was worshipped there in the form of a huge serpent. [As a form of Nut, she was the female counterpart of the serpent god Nau, just like the Samael and Lilith stories. The Serpent in this story was a monster.]*

Once you make all types of vicious and powerful animals and you manipulate the genetic codes by splicing in human DNA into others to make "half-human soldiers, the next thing to do would be going to war. While it was a long time ago, there is evidence that Nuclear exchanges occurred during the second entry of massive dinosaurs. Some of the dinosaur bones they have been finding over the last few decades are so radio-active that they must be painted with special leaded paint to reduce the levels to a safety for visitors to see them in museums, but that is not the only proof. What if some dinosaurs weren't fossilized?

Dinosaur Reconstruction

There were problems with Dinosaur remains. As I mentioned, some were found with high levels of radiation which didn't fit the ancient Cretaceous destruction, but then something else started making us change our minds about massive beasts we though had been extinct. Some are now claiming that dinosaurs were not running around even hundreds of thousands of years ago. Instead, at least some, were only very recently living on earth and may have died just before the Pleistocene Extinction. This statement is both true and false. It was as if some of the dinosaurs made it past the Cretaceous Extinction, or SOMEONE remade these dinosaurs from DNA samples from the Cretaceous. To look into this oddness, we need to look at soft tissue.

Soft Tissue Not Fossilized

Sometimes the mineral deposits are working fine, but there is a true anomaly until an answer is presented. They have found soft tissue [un-fossilized stuff] inside some of the dinosaur bones.

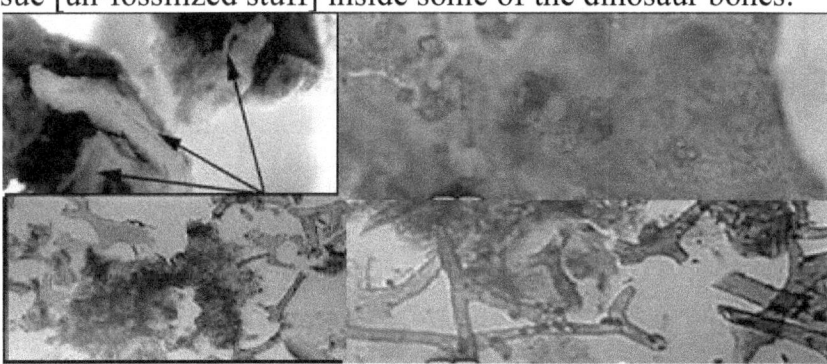

Less than 50 Thousand Years Old

While the geologists were squabbling, there has been pretty much consensus that soft tissues must be less than 50 thousand years old. Most say if the insides are less than 50 thousand years old the dinosaur that died must have lived less than 50 thousand years ago. They have been finding soft tissue since 2007 and more continues.

More Biological Material Found

As of April 2014, in fossils from dinosaur-layer and deeper strata, researchers have discovered flexible and transparent blood vessels, red blood cells, many various proteins including the microtubule building block tubulin, collagen, the cytoskeleton component actin, and hemoglobin, bone maintenance osteocyte cells, and powerful evidence for DNA. Blood vessels from a T-Rex are shown below.

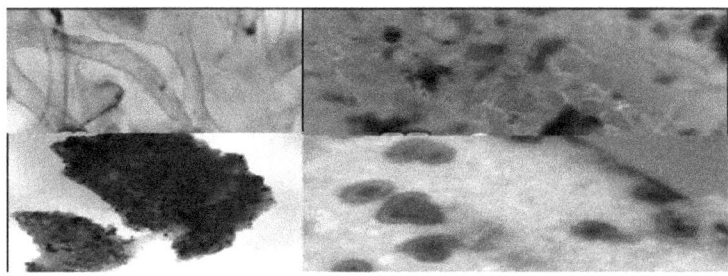

The list of dinosaurs that were, apparently remade during the Pleistocene keep growing and now include; Hadrosaur, titanosaurs, mosasaur, triceratops, ornithomimosaur, Lufengosaurs, T. Rex, and Archaeopteryx.

Triceratops, Hadrosaur, and T-Rex

Triceratops and Hadrosaur bones from Montana were tested for Carbon 14 two different dating labs both said that the triceratops registered an average of 31,000 radiocarbon years and 23,000 years was the date for the Hadrosaur. Some researchers cut open a number of T-Rex bones and found masses of soft material that had not fossilized yet. Meaning the animal was probably less than 50,000 years old. The scientific community went berserk. This was a lie; this was a mistake; this was an anomaly. Soon all the back pointing was of no use as more and more finds showed the same thing. Some T-Rexs lived well past the time of the reported extinction. An example of the elastic material is shown below.

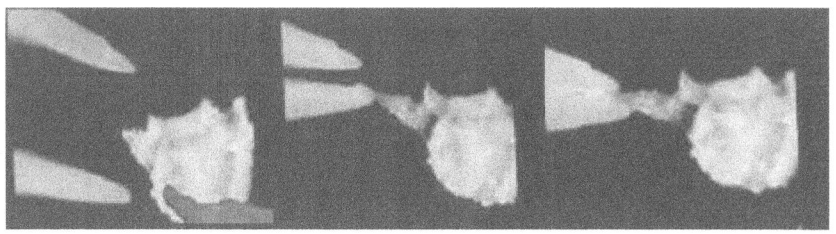

Young Smilodon

Recent radiocarbon dating done <u>on collagen</u> that was taken from " femur bones" of twelve extinct saber tooth tigers, from the LeBrea Tar Pits of Los Angeles California ranged from 12,650 to 28,000 years before the present. Oops!!!

I thought everything died during the great extinction!!!

There is no question that the K-T chalk barrier marks a massive extinction. The T-Rex, Triceratops, Hadrosaur, and possibly even the Smilodon, would have been on the list of extinction receivers. The new evidence is almost irrefutable, so something happened? These animals were manufactured before the great Cretaceous extinction period. -----Then---- <u>they were re-made</u> well after the end of the Cretaceous period. We know the scientists of that time were well ahead of us in many technologies including genetic manipulation. It would have been easy to reestablish any of the dinosaurs desired if DNA had been stored or if viable DNA was found on dead animals of that time. We even find out that they were re-created again AFTER the Pleistocene Extinction.

Who Made New Dinosaurs?

Some will come up to you and claim the earth is only a couple thousand years old because some of the dinosaurs have been found that were not completely fossilized. There are countless writings on the regeneration of animals into something the Bible called "Unclean" or Abominable" animals. I have picked out a few to reinforce this substantial event that has greatly mystified geo-historians, religious historians, and just about everyone else. The details are clear as you will see. The Anak scientists were the surviving rebels from what the Bible calls the Heaven War which happened just before the Earth became void and without form as stated in the second part of the first chapter of Genesis along with many, many other places. According to ancient texts, the Anak people had "special" knowledge including the working of Iron, building of war machines, modifying animals, and even flight. Here are some of the examples of what was said about the making of animals [Dinosaurs in particular for this book]

Just about everywhere you look, we find that animals were genetically modified including Dinosaurs. Some may have even been regenerated after the worldwide flood.

Enoch 7:5-6 *And the ANAK began to* *sin against birds, and beasts, and reptiles, and fish,* *and to devour one another's flesh, and drink the blood.*

Enoch 10:10-11-Restore the Earth, which the Nephilim have corrupted; and announce life to it, that I may revive it. All the sons of men shall not perish in consequence of every secret, by which the Angels have destroyed, and which *they have taught their offspring.* ***All the Earth has been corrupted*** *by the effects of the teachings of Azazyal* *[This*

Jubilees 4:8- And lawlessness increased on the earth and *all flesh corrupted its way,* *alike men and cattle and beasts and birds and everything that walks on the earth -all of them corrupted their ways and their orders,* *---7:3- And after this* *[The war] they* *sinned against the beasts and birds.* *[*There are two ways to sin against beasts- sex and genetic manipulation. The corrupted animals were known as "unclean" monsters. All reptiles were in this unclean animal list.]

Jasher 4:18-19 and the sons of men in those days took from the cattle of the Earth, the beasts of the field and the fowls of the air, and *taught the mixture of animals of one species with the other,* *in order therewith to provoke the Lord; and God saw the whole Earth and it was corrupt, for all flesh had corrupted its ways upon Earth, all men and* *all animals..* [Corrupted animals did not mean the animals were evil, it meant that the species were changed inappropriately.]

Book of Naphtali 1:25-26- The Gentiles went astray, and forsook the Lord and *changed their order,* *and obeyed stocks and stones,* *spirits of deceit—become not as <u>Sodom, which changed the order of nature</u>*. [Nephilim and gentiles practiced genetic manipulation]

***II Enoch 59:5-6**- But whosoever kills a beast without wounds, kills his own soul and defiles his flesh. <u>And he who does any beast any injury whatsoever, in secret, it is evil practice, and he defiles his own soul</u>.* [The killing and injury done in secret was not killing animals for food, it was, most likely, genetic manipulation]

***Book of Creation**-Samael [Satan] said," I have no need for anyone-it is I who am God, and there is no other one that exists from me"---Pisitis [**God**] was filled with anger and said " You are mistaken, Samael, there is an immortal man of light that has been in existence before you, and who will appear <u>amid the creatures you have made,</u> and will trample you, and you will descend to the abyss--- then he and his followers made a great war in the seven heavens.* [Like the Sumerian version, Satan and his cohorts designed animal monsters to fight in another Heaven War. Many of the monsters he designed were huge dinosaurs.]

More Finds Every Year

Biological Material Found as of December 2015: Researchers have discovered flexible and transparent blood vessels, red blood cells, many various proteins including the microtubule building block tubulin, collagen, the cytoskeleton components actin, tropomyosin, and the related motor protein myosin, and hemoglobin, bone maintenance osteocyte cells, pigment and evidence of melanosomes, DNA-related histone proteins, and powerful evidence for DNA including positive results from multiple double-helix tests. Soft pliable skin is now being found as shown below.

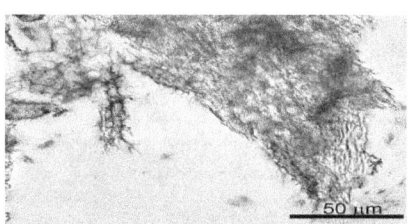

Carbon-14 Found in dinosaur fossils- Now Carbon 14 decays in only thousands of years, but it has been found in coal, oil,

79

limestone, fossil wood, graphite, natural gas, marble and now, dinosaur fossils.IN 2011 They started finding C14 in Mosasaurs and now it's everywhere.

In 2005 Exceptionally preserved sauropod were eggshells discovered in what was believed to be Cretaceous age rock, but they contained skeletal remains and soft tissues of embryonic Titanosaurid dinosaurs.

Naturally-pigmented Tyrannosaurus Rex images depict tissue containing osteocytes and interconnected, flexible, transparent vessels similar to modern vessels.

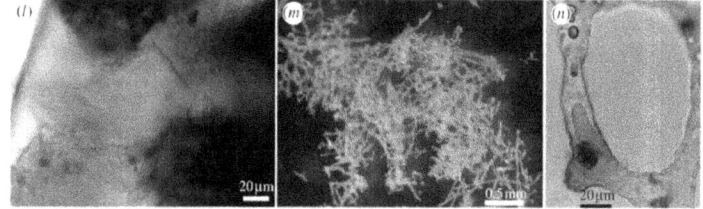

Duck-bill Dinosaurs with soft tissue- Some flexible from a leg bone is shown below.

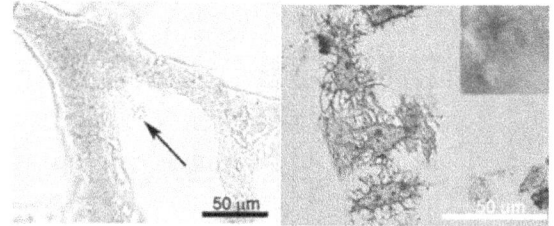

Way back in 1954 – paleobiologists found amino acids that supposedly lived before the Mesozoic. It was disregarded as impossible. After only 60 years most are realizing dinosaurs were here during the Pleistocene.

Land Dinosaurs Survived

As amazing as the soft tissue dinosaur remain is, we can be pretty sure some of the huge monsters survived, were recreated, or remanufactured after the massive shift in the earth that ended the Pleistocene Age and flooded the world. You can't keep a good geneticist down and the scientists of the day began recreating dinosaurs that were smaller and more tolerant versions. Most of the newer dinosaurs were slightly smaller, but generally they were still quite scary and those in the oceans were still pretty huge. While other things were going on as I explained earlier, some of the animals miraculously survived the flood and, of course, some of the ancient humans survived. What we find is that earth could no longer support the really massive land giants Substantial evidence shows there were reduced size monsters here 3 thousand years ago---or less. Two of these animals are listed in Jewish histories. These were the Leviathan and Behemoth. The Behemoth was the land variant.

Behemoth

In the centuries that followed the Heaven Wars, some of the smaller dinosaurs and other large creatures must have survived or were regenerated. I know that doesn't sound right after I went to all the trouble of establishing the extinction of dinosaurs 65 million years ago as the earth's spin began to slow down and the dinosaurs simply got too heavy to survive, but thousands of years ago depictions of these creatures were captured. In Mexico and in Peru images of men with dinosaurs were drawn. As shown on the left below, in Peru, images of dinosaurs were often put on clay while clay models of dinosaurs and dragon-like creatures were molded in ancient Mexico, as shown on the right.

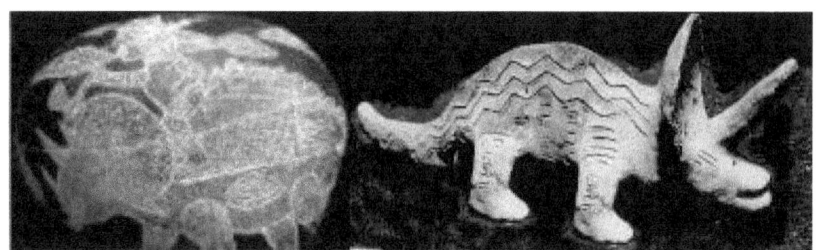

Additionally, many stories of the dragons were left by the ancient writers and artists from around the world. The images and stories indicate that, not only did the Earth inhabitants walk with dinosaurs during the Cretaceous Age, but humans were in company of Dragons and similar creatures up until at least 3 thousand years ago. Confrontation probably did not always have a present outcome. Some of the creatures called Dragons, I'm not going to go into the hundreds of stories about Dragons from all parts of the world in the history, but it should be sufficient to say that the existence or memory of those magnificent creatures was well known during ancient times. Below are some more of the pictures found in Peru which show that dinosaurs were still alive during much of the post-flood era. The one on the left was a depiction found in a cave while the depiction on the right was a huge depiction inscribed in the Nazca Plain of Peru. One thing to note about the depiction on the Nasca Plain is that the drawing had to be done after the worldwide flood 10 thousand years ago. If it was drawn before the flood, it would have completely washed away.

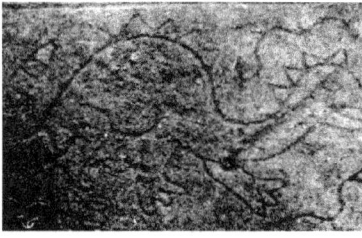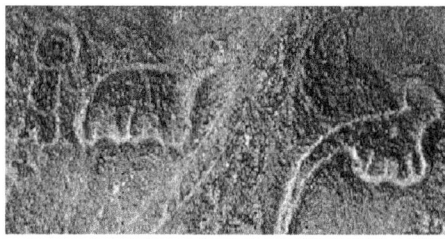

What these images and the hundreds of other similar ones show is not a mystery or an anomaly, it simply shows that genetics was mastered by people who survived the flood and recreated smaller versions of dinosaurs that "sometimes could be domesticated to some degree.

> *Man almost certainly saw smaller versions of dinosaurs well after the dinosaurs were supposedly extinct at the end of the Cretaceous and that means there is a likelihood that some still exist..*

It should be noted that even the Bible recounted dinosaurs surviving until about 3 thousand years ago. That means they survived the dinosaur extinction, and the worldwide flood. On land another dinosaur survivor was certainly noticed all over the world at that time it was called Dragon or Behemoth. Here are a few of the texts that describe these monsters.

II Esdras 6:48-Then he set apart two creatures the Behemoth and the Leviathan. You put them in separate places. The country of 1000 hills was given to behemoth. [A few dinosaurs survived.]

Job 40:15-24- Behold now behemoth, which I made with thee; he eateth grass as an ox. His strength is in his loins, and his force is in the navel of his belly. He moveth his tail like a cedar [There are no cedar tailed hippos, but the huge Diplodocus dinosaur had a tail worthy of mentioning]: The sinews of his stones are wrapped together. His bones are as strong pieces of brass; his bones are like bars of iron. He is the chief of the ways of God: He lieth under the shady trees, in the cover of the reed, and ferns. Behold, he drinketh up a river, and hasteth not: He taketh it with his eyes: his nose pierceth through snares.

San Antonio Behemoth

As far as more modern representations of the behemoth or land dinosaur, let's look at one that was killed in San Antonio Texas in 1997. Supposedly the rancher that killed the 5 foot long beast indicated that it kept on killing his chickens and even a donkey. The dinosaur had two-fingered hands and a rigid back spines along its entire back. [Next Left]

Palestrina Behemoth

This mosaic done around 100AD shows a very impressive behemoth being attacked. Maybe they were hunted like other animals a couple of thousand years ago. [Right]

83

Anasazi Behemoth

A very clear petroglyph of a dinosaur found at Natural Bridges National Monument in Utah. It is attributed to the Anasazi Indians who lived in the area from AD 400 to AD 1300. The image show a diplodocus like monster with a human nearby as shown below.

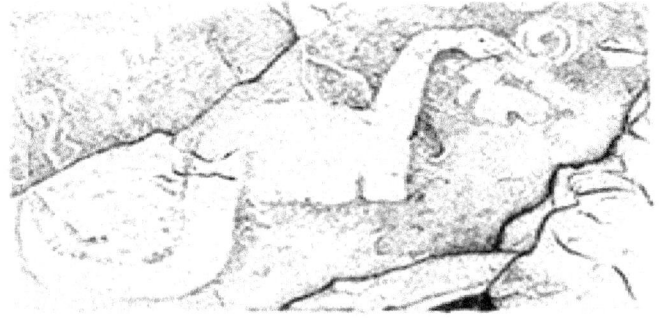

French Behemoth

Pictured below is a rock carving from Bernifal Cave in France. It shows a head-to-head confrontation between a dinosaur and a mammoth. Although this carving cannot be dated, it is clearly from the post-Flood period, but still a long time ago. Clearly these monsters survived for many years or were recreated after the Pleistocene Extinction.

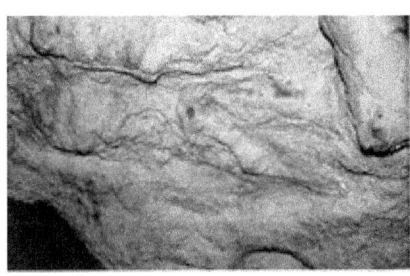

Greek Behemoth

The image below clearly shows people fighting an ancient behemoth. Most of the people of that time had never read about dinosaurs so their image of these creatures came from actual encounters. In this case, looks like the dinosaur is losing. The ANAK had created or recreated these animals during their reign on earth. Their reign lasted thousands of years with the help of something that kept them alive thousands of years. Greeks called it Ambrosia, and the Jews thought that it was similar to pomegranate. There is another possibility.

Age Tubes

Now we come to a very important element. One of the reasons that the ANAK people could make all these animals and become like gods to the normal people of the day is that they lived a long, long, long time. How did these guys stay young for thousands and thousands of years? Certainly that is a myth, you might think, but the ambrosia of the Greek Gods, and the tree of life fruit for Adam and Eve and other fruit was reportedly used by many of these guys well after the flood. Some indicated that the tree of life fruits were unavailable after the flood and they still didn't get older until after the Tower of Babel or Bharata War incident 6000 years ago. It wasn't until that time that, all of a sudden, people started dying even before they became 200 years old. What had happened? To keep the ANAK young, it appears they came up with artificial means.

What do Apes, Egypt, and Electricity have in common? The answer or at least the question is found on pictures in a temple in Dendera are shown in the following section. These pictures depict something people like to call the Dendera tube. Two of these devices are shown on the following page. The devices appear to be electronic and apes are depicted with them. I'll get to the apes later as we determine how there could be ape-like monsters seen around the world. Right now noticed that these tubes are well protected and revered by those identified as gods. What do you suppose they would revere so much. My guess is an artificial tree of life fruit.

If that was the only depiction, no one would think too much about it, but more and more were found. The following group of pictures next depict some type of electronic tube-like objects resting on still other strange devices. These are all held up by a little human who tries to point the main device at a **baboon**. That's right; a baboon. The baboon character here was very important to the society.

Dendera Tube and Electricity

I've got to tell you that these "Dendera tubes", by their very looks, must have used some kind of electricity. The twisted cabling to their base, the filament like internal structure, and the radiation type insulator holding the one on the right following all point to the same conclusion. I don't want to get into in this book, but let me just say, the ANAK had electricity. There is no doubt about it and plenty of proof.

The electricity would have been used to make these things radiate in some way. The radiating component produced something special. There is something else you should recognize. There is a miniaturized image of Pharaoh under the left Dendera tube on both of the first two carvings. This indicates that the pharaoh needed whatever this machine produced and the pharaoh was insignificant with respect to the Dendera Tube or the ANAK giants. In the third image following is only different in that the Pharaoh is under the one on the right. These things must have been really something to be more important that a pharaoh. The 2nd and last images show a huge baboon guard wielding a knife, evidently to protect the Dendera tubes, so here is my theory, for what it's worth.

Maybe the thing had something to do with keeping the demigod rulers [like pharaoh] alive after the tree of life was lost in the worldwide flood. The Baboons were hired to make sure most people did not live as long as the rulers.

Here is the obvious statement. If you hired baboons to guard this most valuable thing, the must have been quasi-human baboons around at the time. Again I'll explain later.

As one would expect, the ANAK in Egypt were not the only ones that wanted to live a long time. These things started showing up everywhere. The ANAK and the ANAKIM were using these things, presumably to keep from growing old.

More Life Devices

Sumerian Radiators

Not only do we find these things in Egypt, we find them around the world. Read the section below from the "Epic of Gilgamesh" and see if this could have been describing the Dendera Tube energy.

Sumerian Epic of Gilgamesh- *Upon the corpse, hung from the pole, they* ***directed the pulse and the radiance****; 60 times the water of life, 60 times the food of life, they sprinkled upon it; and Inanna arose* **[Sounds like some kind of electric shock treatment, used to bring Innana back to life. Could the pictured apparatus have been the device used to deliver the directed pulse??]**

Picture of the Device

We may have a picture of the ancient Sumerian form of this device. On this seal can be seen a tube with some kind of rays emanating away from it. The device looks very much like the Dendera Tubes. We can call this one the "Sumerian Tube". The only difference is that fish men have replaced the baboon and one of the dozens of depicted flying machines is flying overhead. Really good Dendera tunes might even have flying ships with multiple people riding as this Sumerian seal implies. Only one fish guy is shown here[left 2], but the depictions are always the same.

Assyrian Radiating Tubes

89

Here are some examples [above right 2] of the Assyrian version. In this depiction, the radiator seems to have fruit making it more probable that the ANAK made artificial "Tree-of-Life fruit with the device. A Merkaba [Flying Machine] is still dancing overhead just like in the Sumerian version. The men have changed clothes, but the rest is the same. The Assyrian artifact flowers and Cherubimic eagle-headed ANAK pick the fruit. This could have been showing that the Dendera tube was an artificial Tree-of-Life.

Aztec   Radiators-The Aztecs and Mayans both depicted "radiating tubes" of some kind. Something shoots out of the Aztec version while the Mayan one shows an internal filament similar to the Dendera tubes of Egypt. The Aztecs must also have known about this device as well. The Codex Nuttal shows the device [next left]. Some kind of radiating beam is coming from the central orb. The device is standing by what appears to be a rocket and a throne. No people are in this section of the work, nor are there any baboons, but a baboon was one of the Aztec gods.

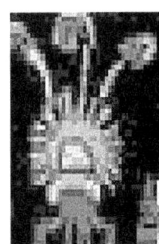  

Guatemala Radiators-The Mayans also depicted a radiating tube of some kind as shown in this page of the Dresden Codex. [middle above] I don't know what the snake thing is in the foreground either.

Indian Radiators-In India a similar radiating tube was depicted, but this one seems to be somewhat different in that a person gets inside the tube. It certainly was no simple light bulb. [Above Right] Apes didn't simply protect this Dendera thing; some were important people of the community and even were revered as gods. Let's see what else the ape-men were up to.

Ape Monsters

Here come a tricky subject. Sasquatch! This monster certainly can't be real, because it simply makes no sense. How could a throw-back like that still exist. If it makes no sense, it must be nonsense.

Wait Just a minute!!!!!

We need a little more history here. Everyone has heard about the Tower of Babel, but what you might not know is that the Tower was destroyed as part of a massive worldwide war that was described by many people in many nations around the world. Parts of the world were almost completely destroyed, fortifications and cities were melts from the extreme heat of the weaponry of the day. The book of Jasher tells us that 1/3 of the population of the world died in the war and a second 1/3 of the population <u>became like APES</u>. The remaining people were scattered around the world. The city of Mohen-jo-Daro in India still holds dozens of skeleton remains of radioactive dead. We can't begin to understand just how horrible the war was, but you must understand that this war did in fact happen and something else happened.

The Bible tells us that people could no longer communicate with friends, the preMaya wrote that people forgot just about everything they once knew. On and on we can go an find that an age of primitive living was about to unfold on the earth. Whether that happened because of a release "germ" during the war or other accident, it is not known, but some of the people were affected tremendously and they became more ape than human in appearance. You don't have to believe me on this, but do believe the massive amount of physical evidence as many ape-people became critical to the civilization around the world just after this event. Here are a few

Egyptian Ape-men

The Egyptians believed in a baboon god. While we are on the subject of an ape-man being the god named Thoth, we also need to go around the world including Mexico and Cambodia and investigate a similar strangeness. Many places worshipped these hairy humanoids, which may or may not help us understand what happened to some of the people after the Tower of Babel incident. At least it will show how revered the ape-man was. We might not completely understand what the ancient historians meant by telling us about the transformation from human to ape-like human, but one thing is certain. Around the world there were apes that were very humanlike. They came on the sense around 5 thousand years ago and were completely gone from the earth by 3 thousand years ago. Humanlike ape-men were depicted as worshiping some type of orb at a higher level than the humans. They were certainly not depicted as animals. [**The orb could be another one of those Dendera tubes-- Next left.]**

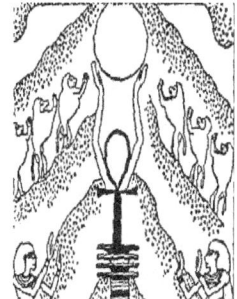 

Bird headed Ape-men

Sometimes the Egyptian ape-men turned partially into birds, but they still could defeat humans and evidently did by this depiction. [Above right]

The Aztec Ape-men

The Aztecs have Quetzalcoatl. Like the Egyptian ape-gods, he was a baboon and a human. There is a fairly high probability that Thoth and Quetzalcoatl were the same demigod flying around in his ship between the new world and Egypt. Here is a picture of the Aztec version. Maybe Thoth brought the knowledge of his electric device with him. Maybe Thoth got zapped during the Babel Incident.

*Panama Ape-men-*Mayans were no different than the Aztecs. They also worshipped apes. This effigy is in the form of a footstool or platform. [Second Above]

*Maya Ape-men-*In Ecuador, this monkey-man was revered. Why would the ancient people of Ecuador revered this backward looking half human unless some of the leaders were monkey-like? [Above right]

*The Cambodian Ape People-*The ancient capital city of Cambodia is called Ankor-Watt. Similar Ape-men appear to be guarding the entrances to the temples—Who knows? [See next left]

Indian Monkey Gods

In Indian history, Monkey-men soldiers fought along the side of their hero Rama. Rama was battling his brother who was evil. Smoke is billowing out of two of the monkeys shown. I don't know what it means, but from the looks of their wounds, they were in trouble. The one with 12 holes is Rama. [Above middle] In Sri Lanka, and ape-man by the name of Hunaman, became the savior of the city. His image is to the right above.

Anakim Gods

After the nasty war, things were different. Much of the prehistory knowledge was lost forever, Ape-like people were all over the place, and the ANAK [giant long headed people] were getting old as the Dendera tubes quit working. The world was being taken over by a newer group called the Anakim or "sons of the ANAK". Let's see if we can find some of the Anakim as these guys continued to experiment with animals for some time and to keep alive the more ancient breeds of monsters that amused them. While the ANAK had been huge, the Anakim were no slouchers, whenever the Jews first saw some of these guys they became terribly fearful and indicated that they were the size of grasshoppers compared to the ANAKIM.

In the March 2001 National Geographic- The article titled "Tomb of Giants" provides a depiction of "giants" in a Moche burial in Peru. To the right is a general size comparison of some of the strange giants compared to a "normal skeleton. Clearly this was a different race of individuals than the "Normal" humans. [See graphic next left]

Skull Evidence-Even the skulls were different. Some time ago, a large quantity of skulls from what must have been large humans was found. The creatures were human to be sure, but look at the skulls pictured below Right. Look at the long skinny head and the heavy jaw. There was no mistake that these "humans were of a different species than the other humans that lived in the area. Still more show similar traits The last guy probably had the biggest trepanation surgery ever performed and notice that he lived many years after the surgery as the skull had begun to heal.

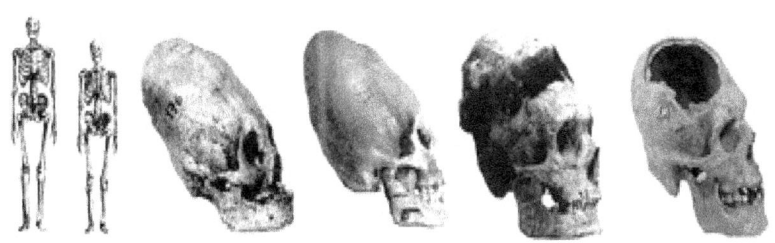

The next to the last above must have been a character. He had a bandana around his head so tight that it indented his skull. The pronounced chin characterizes these "humans" with the Cro-Magnon humans that had miraculously appeared at the beginning of the Pleistocene Age in the Middle East, but these ANAK and Anakim giants weren't like the other Cro-Magnon type humans at all.

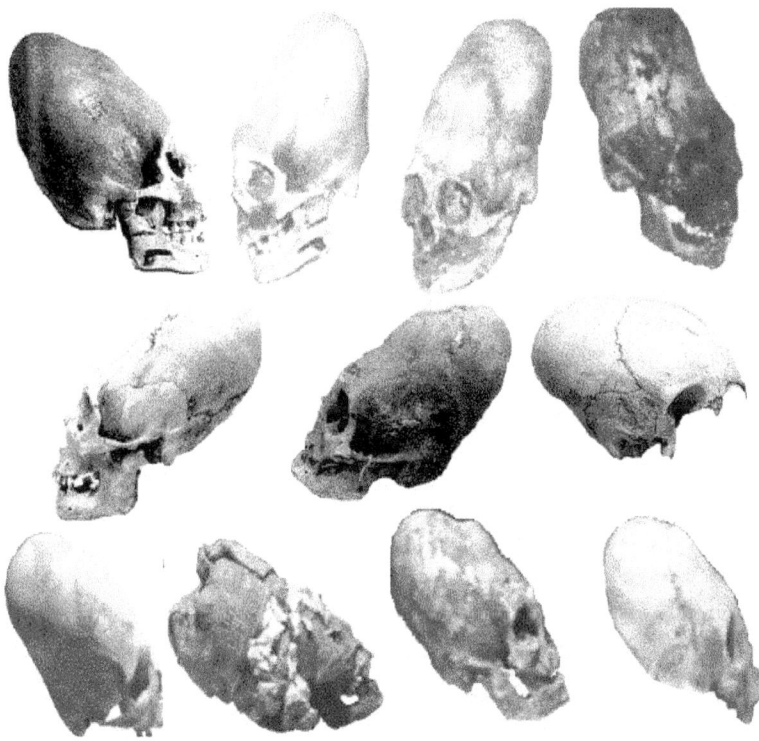

They were considered gods and people from around the world tried to mimic the long skinny head by tying bands around their heads and many other things to try to deform children's skulls to the more pleasing long-head [Anakim] shape. Not only were long headed giant rulers found in the Americas, but also in Europe.

95

Here are some specific finds from France, England, and Switzerland.

French Anakim Monster makers

French Evidence-In the 17th century, in a sand quarry in southern France workers found the remains of a huge giant. Eighteen feet down, the workers found a coffin 30 feet long, 12 feet wide and 8 feet deep. Inside were the bones of a giant no less than 25 feet tall. Its skull, was 5 feet long and he had six toes on each foot. Estimated age by the coffin depth was about 10 thousand years old.

More French Evidence-In another report we find a similar type of human. "Skulls found in the Dordogne Valley, France showed a most significant trait—**long heads** and broad faces."

Still More French Evidence-23-foot tall skeleton found in 1456 A.D. beside a river in Valence, France.

More French Evidence-A 25' 6 " skeleton found in 1613 A.D. near the castle of Chaumont in France. This was claimed to be a nearly complete find.

These Frenchmen really found some monstrous giants.

English Anakim

English Evidence-In an old book entitled "History And Antiquities Of Allerdale," there is an account of a giant found in Cumberland, England, at an unknown date in the Middle Ages. Called "A True Report of Hugh Hodson, of Thorneway," it states: *"The said giant was buried four yards deep in the ground, which is now a corn field. He was four yards and a half long, and was in complete armor; his sword and battle-axe lying by him....his teeth were six inches long, and two inches broad...."*

Roman Evidence-Maximinus Thrax Ceaser of Rome 235-238 A.D. This was an 8' 6" skeleton.

Switzerland Evidence-A huge skull was found in Switzerland. It was perfectly formed similar to Cro-Magnon, except it was immense **and the head was long**.

German Evidence [The Giants of the Cave]- This is an account from 1535 of 25 men who entered the Breitenwinner Cave to find something might strange. Like places around the world, Giants were forced to live underground. This must have been one of the underground cities. *"- We started very early -- we came upon a wide space like a hall for dancing. - we found so many bones. The bones were very large as if from giants. At [380 m] one comes into -a beautiful spacious palace -- Here we found two skulls which to our surprise were enclosed by the rock, we could hardly hack them out with our tools. There were many passages ---and passages were full of big bones. -- We arrived at another wide space -- like a chapterhouse, with pews on one wall and a gallery overhead.--. In all the caves we found many bones. We came to a narrow vault where we found a skull bigger than we had ever seen before. When we tried to squeeze it through the narrow opening it crumbled like ashes--. Adjoining this wide cave was a handsome triangular vault. There we found a stone sculpture. It resembled a deity seated on a throne -- We found another stone sculpture hanging from a high wall. --We found loose soil with a great many bones. We came to a most wonderful palace and tabernacle."*---[finally they team left the 1700meter deep cave.]

More German Anakim- Long skulls were found in Germany. About 20 of those like the one shown below left attest to a strong colony of Anakim rulers there.

Alaskan Anakim-From the Aleutian Islands, one of the massive skulls found there was sent back to the Smithsonian for study. At one time, it was believed to have held the largest human brain at about 70% more massive than current humans [similar to what was found in South America. The Alaskan Anakim is shown next to a "normal skull". Researchers would go on to find over 100 of these remains in various parts of the United States.

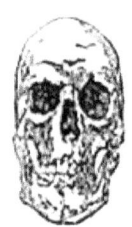   

Russian Anakim- Long Anakim skulls were found all over in Siberia just like in Germany, Peru, USA, and just about everywhere else around the globe. An example is shown below right.

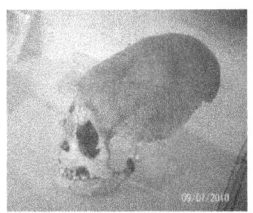 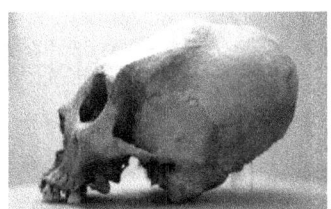

Jewish Historian Description-Flavius Josephus, the noted Jewish historian of the first century A.D., described the giants as having *"bodies so large and countenances so entirely different from other men that they were surprising to the sight and terrible to the hearing."* And he adds that in his day, the bones of the giants were still on display!

Additional Biblical Testimony- There are many Biblical texts describing the giant overlords of the day. Here is one talking about those who rule the land of Canaan. *"All the people we saw in it were men of great stature. And there we saw the the sons of Anak, who descended from the Nephilim: and we seemed to ourselves as grasshoppers, and so did we to them"* (Numbers 13:32-33).

Goliath was about 9 feet + or - a few inches. *I Samuel 17:4.*

King Og spoken of in Deuteronomy 3:11 whose iron bedstead was approximately 14-feet by 6-feet wide. King Og was at least 12-feet tall, yet some claim up to 18 feet.

Turkey-In the late 1950's during road construction in Homs southeast Turkey, many tombs of Giants were reportedly unearthed. These tombs were 4 meters long. During exhumation, the skeletal remains were examined. The human thigh bones were measured to be 47.24 inches in length. They calculated that the person who owned this Femur probably stood at fourteen to sixteen feet tall as shown to the right. A cast of this bone is seen at the Creationist museum in Texas. [Next Left]

Egyptian Long Head Rulers-Let's briefly look at the heads of the early Egyptian leaders for comparison. In the early days, this land was known as the land of Kemet. While we don't have the heads of the ancient leaders, we do have head sculptures. Just like the rulers of the ancient preInca, the rulers of Kemet had the characteristic long heads of the Anakim. [Next Right]

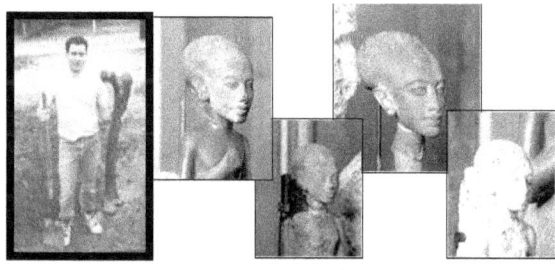

These long headed demigod scientists continued to build animals by all accounts because they are still everywhere. The Anakim died off about 3500 years ago, but some of the monsters lived on. Don't ignore the evidence just because it doesn't fit into your idea of what life is supposed to be like. Monsters survived the Cretaceous Extinction, the Pleistocene Extinction, the Tower of Babel War, and they are still around. Let's look at some of the evidence.

Modern Monsters

If these monsters lived during the ancient times and during the times of the ANAKIM could they still be lurking in different parts of the world? Of course the answer is yes and in fact, MANY have been spotted over the years. Some of these you will recognize and others may seem less known, but I think you will see that many monsters still roam the earth. Misfits of forgotten wars and miscreated animals of a once great society. I'm not talking about all the animals identified as abominations, but certainly the group of monsters defined as vile---- the reptile

99

monsters. There are some other special ones we will not leave off as well, but let's see what we have. Our first encounter will be with unbelievable huge, dangerous and monstrous serpents. I don't mean the normal Boa Constrictors and Anacondas seen in zoos and written about, I'm talking about snakes as large as a 5 to 10 story building. This type of monster has both the demeanor to ingest humans, but some have certainly had that fate. After the snake review, we will looks at evidence of Giant Kraken, Dragon-like flying reptiles, Behemoth like land monsters, Many, Leviathan like sea monsters, and the remaining members of the ape-men populations from around the world. It's not a pretty world out there and for us to sit back and simply say these monsters do not exist is just wrong.

Giant Snake Monsters

A small piece of a relatively large snake is shown below. A nice man models to show how many people could fit inside its belly.

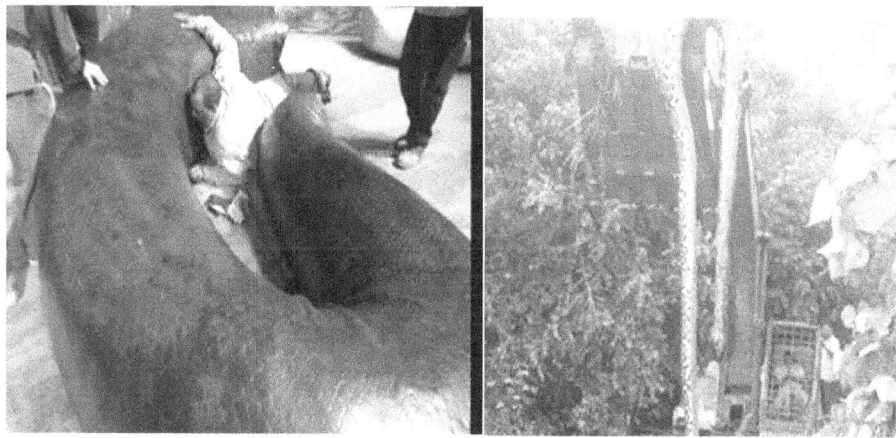

In China, modern machinery was able to lift this 60 foot long serpent monster after its eventual death. No telling how many buffalo, small animals and possibly even humans were on his menu. Just think of a land animal longer than most whales.

In 1959, a British pilot was flying over Katanga and spotted another 60 foot long serpent. He took the picture below as evidence of his enormous find. No one had to get a tape measure to know that this guy was huge. The small trail on the right side of the picture possibly was a roadway. A close up is shown to the right..

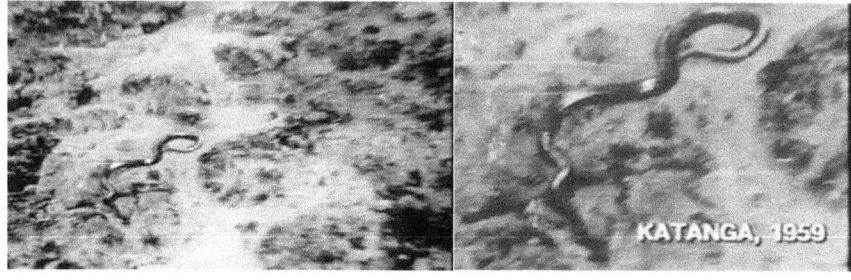

If you thought that was a fluke, below are other similar finds. While most are found in Africa, that does not mean that giant serpent monsters are isolated to that region of the world. Please don't feed these snakes as they soon will feed on you.

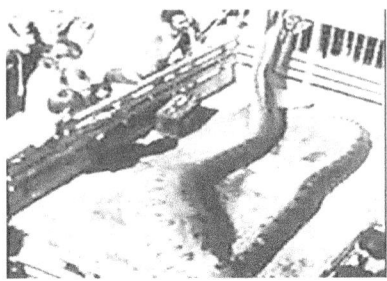

An eye witness account is no more comforting. This comes from Colonel Fawcett, of the Royal Engineers."*I sprang for my rifle as the creature began to make its way up the bank and smashed a .44 bullet into its spine. At once there was a flurry of foam and several heavy thumps against the boats keel, shaking us as though we had run on a snag. We stepped ashore and approached the creature with caution. As far as it was possible to measure, a length of 45 feet lay out of the water and 17 feet lay in the water, making it a total length of 62 feet. It's body was not thick, not more than 12 inches in diameter, but it had probably been long without food.*"

Here is another from Bernard Huevelmans, and his encounter with a group of Frenchmen and Brazilians. "*We saw the snake asleep in a large patch of grass. We immediately opened fire upon it. It tried to make off all in convulsions but we caught up with it and finished it off. Only then did we realize how enormous it was, when we walked around the whole length of its body it seemed like it would never end. What struck me was its enormous head, a triangle about 24 inches by 20. We had no instruments to measure the beast, but we took an arm's length of string and measured it about one meter by placing it on a man's shoulder and extending it to his fingertips. We measured the snake several times and each time we got a length of 25 strings. The creature was well over 23 meters or 75 feet long.*"

Still another from Father Victor Heinz gives us a picture of this monster in 1925 Amazon. *"The visible portion was at least 80 feet long and the body was as thick as an oil drum. It was throwing up a wake as large as a river.*

The photo in the middle was recently released from unknown sources in Borneo, depicting the weirdest of occurrences – a 100 foot-long snake-like creature cruising in the waters of the Baleh river.

Badigui Snake-In 1928 a snakelike animal called Ngakoula-ngou or Badigui was reported in the Ubangi-Shari area. [above right]

1555 Snake- Giant Snake was drawn by Olaus Magnus's in 1555 as shown, below left.

Ular tedong Snake- Known as Ular Tedong or simply the naga, this monster appears to be a giant Cobra-like monster in Lake Tasek Bera. It is said they have large scales and are grey or golden in color. They are said to be vegetarian, make a loud booming sound, and are huge.

Lenox Globe Snakes-On the Hunt-Lenox Globe dating from the early 1500s, there is a notation near the East coast of China that reads HC SUNT DRACONES Here are Dragons and giant snakes are shown in the foreground, as shown above right.

The Kraken

Loose the Kraken, the Greek history indicated. A giant tenticled monster rose from the sea to cause havoc. Many, many ancient accounts of this terrible monster tell us that some of these giant squid being found today were making life bad for those near the sea. Images shown describe the terror of these things.

Connecticut Kraken—This was written July 18, 1895 by Capt. Obadiah Donaldson, whose crew allegedly fought off a 60-foot-wide octopus with 100-foot-long arms after accidentally crashing into it. *"He was in a deep sleep, and his snores could be heard quite a way off. --I had no wish to fight him. He darted at us, kicking up the sea. One of his long arms came aboard and seized the forward steam windlass. He wound his arm around it, thinking, I suppose, that it was a sailor. The mate, with great presence of mind started the windlass, and in less time than it takes to tell it a couple of hundred feet of the arm was wound in,*

and we had the fish a prisoner. But we'd caught a Tartar. He began to pull at the boat, and I was afraid he meant to sink it and eat us at his leisure. The vessel rocked, and I thought she would capsize every minute. I called to Frank Taylor, the boatswain, to cut off the arm and he did so with a meat chopper."

Modern Kraken Attacks- to say Karken aren't around today is a fool's thought. Below is either a portrayal or an unlucky recipient of the karken's pull.

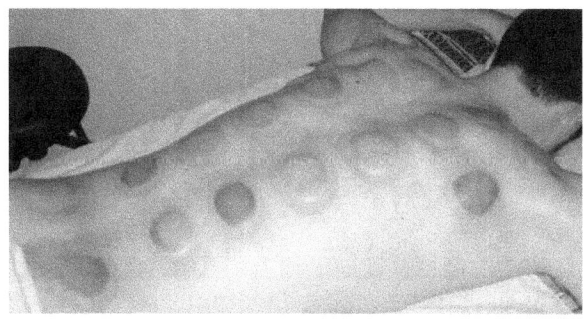

The giant octopus of today are gaining in numbers, coming closer to populations and coming in contact with people with bad results. New reports of these monsters attacking boats, pulling people down into the depths of the ocean, and having huge amount of power and speed allow us to iunderstand the earlier reports were not ficticious or frivolous.

Oklahoma Kraken-Called Oklahoman this lake beast is some type of octopus- or squid-like Kraken, long been feared by the natives of this region. Many disappearances and drownings in the area testify to its meanness. As Squid go it is not an exceptionally large one at about the size of a horse, but still strong enough to kill. With reddish brown leathery skin and tentacles we can assume it is a fresh water version of the Ocean menace.

Whale Eating Kraken-Giant squid or Kraken have been around for millions of years and they are still pretty strange. Many still have the gigantic size associated with the ancient dinosaurs. In bulk, whales are the only being larger and whales love squid, in fact, a study determined that over 70 percent of the food that a sperm whale ate was squid. As you might expect, squid don't like this being eaten thing and larger squid have something that the

105

smaller ones don't have. They have long talons or claws and they hold on with all their might as whales try to suck them inside their bodies. Look at the pictures below of the skin of one such whale. Hundreds of sucker marks typically 4 inches in diameter and talon scratches 2 to 3 meters long typically show the vain struggle of the squids as the whales keep on eating.

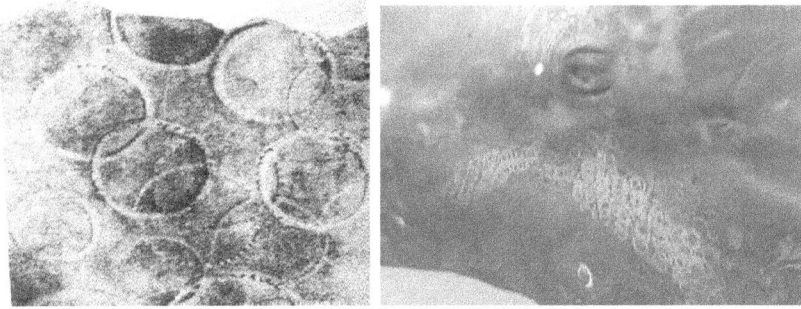

The picture following left shows one of these giants. This is not a huge one, but it certainly is a respectable size. This one is in the process of dying, but majestic and out of place just the same.

"Ancient Humans" practiced Genetic manipulation. These giants were some of the attempts at becoming more powerful. Next is a sequence of a "tiny" giant next to a another diver. [Below right]

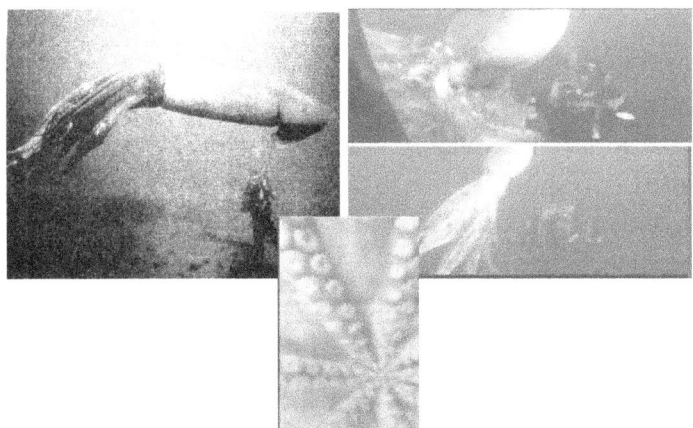

Norway Kraken-It was reported that a Norwegian ship was off the coast of Angola. When getting the unexpected attack, the sailors on the boat and made a vow to St.Thomas is if they can be separated from these dangers, they will perform a pilgrimage. The crew then took an ax and started to fight the monster. The

106

tentacles cut. Monster finally went away. In fulfillment of his vow, the crew then visited the Chapel of St.Thomas in Britanny and hanged a painting [lower right corner of the collage above] as an illustration of the events that befall them.

Denmark Kraken- In this evidence, captain Jean-Magnus Dens from Denmark also met with the creature off the coast of Angola. The giant creature attacking their ships, and even managed to kill three crew. The other crew members did not remain silent and took the gun and fired it into the monster over and over again until he disappeared into the ocean. The captain estimated that monster 35 to 40 feet in length.

Newfoundland Kraken- In October 1873, a fisherman named Theophile Piccot and his son managed to find giant squid tentacles in Newfoundland. Once measured, the researchers concluded that the animal is likely to have a length of up between 35 and 40 feet.

Another French Kraken- In 1875 the Kraken got his eternal enemy, the Sperm Whale. According to the report, in 1875 the eye witness saw a large whale was involved in a great war with a squid that had a body almost as big as whales. The whale was spotted biting squid tentacles systematically. It was believed the Kraken won the fight. To make this story more credible. in the territorial waters of the island in Japan's Bonin, marine researchers managed to get rare photographs showing a whale eating a giant squid that was estimated to have a length of 9 meters. Much of the Kraken was outside the mouth scraping, biting, and using its suckers to stop the hungry whale. In this case, it was believed the squid was not the victor. The collage below shows a very small sampling of the mighty Kraken that have been captured or found on the shore recently.

Speaking of captures, the eye says a lot. Just image an eye the sze shown below. The kraken must have approached 100 feet long.

In 1555 Olaus Magnus wrote of a sea creature with "sharp and long Horns round about, like a tree root up by the roots: They are ten or twelve cubits long, very black, and with huge eyes..." Although the term *kraken* is first found in print in *Systema Naturae* (1735), stories about this monster seem to date back before twelfth century Norway. These tales often refer to a creature so big that it is mistaken for an island or series of islands.

French Kraken- Another story took place on 30 November 1861. When sailing in the Canary Islands, the French crew of the Alencton watched a giant sea monster swimming not far from the ship. The sailors immediately prepared and mortar shells were dropped on the monster. Monster quickly swam away but the ship followed. When they successfully approached, iron forks were thrust into the monster's body and immediately they casted nets.

When the crew lifted the net, the monster's body was badly broken and crushed and fell into the water, leaving only part of the tentacles. The body length of the animal was estimated to be 6 feet without tentacles. Its mass was estimated to be about 2,000 kg. When the ship landed and the tentacles were shown to the scientific community, they agreed that the crew may have witnessed a giant squid with a length of greater than 8 feet. A drawing of the incident was made as shown next left.

Newfoundland Kraken- Giant squid that washed ashore at Trinity Bay, Newfoundland in 1877. The image was published in 'Canadian Illustrated News', October 27, 1877, as shown below right.

13 Ton Kraken- This monster shown was originally thought to be a beached whale. Now some people think it's a *13 ton* octopus/squid/Kraken. Notice the gigantic eye.

1930's Events-On at least three occasions in the 1930's Kraken reportedly attacked a ship. While the squids got the worst of these encounters when they slid into the ship's propellers, the fact that they attacked at all shows that they probably attacked the earlier ships

Ship Sinking-The idea that a giant squid could sink a ship may sound corny today. However, in medieval times, the size of the ship is not as great as we have now. For example, Columbus named Pinta ship had a length of 18 meters [only 60 feet long]. A 10-15 meter long squid was certain to attack and sink the ship with ease.

Modern Dragons

While most of the modern dragon monsters found today are similar to Pterodactyl creatures of the Titan Era, we can assume many types of flying reptiles were made in the past. Some managed to survived until today, but most are killed whenever they are found. As far as I know none have been found to emit fire, however, there are some beetles alive today that do produce fire that is spit out similar to the stories of ancient dinosaurs. One can certainly believe that other animals besides beetle used fire to harm those awakening the beast. Here are just a few of the many sightings of flying dragons.

Egyptian Dragon- Herodotus, describe small flying reptiles in ancient Egypt and Arabia in his history book. He reported that the creatures had a snake-like body and bat-like wings and recorded that he saw a canyon with many piles of their backbones and ribs. He also wrote that the strange creatures could sometimes be found in the spice groves, and that when workers wanted to gather frankincense they would have to make fires with odorous smoke to drive the pesky reptiles away.

Cretean Dragon-Spotted on the Asteroussia Mountains of Crete, this pterosuar-like monster has been seen by several witnesses.

French Dragon-In 1856 in France. Workmen were digging through limestone for a railway tunnel. When a large bolder was split a large winged creature come stumbling out. They said it fluttered its wings, let out a croaking noise and then dropped dead at their feet. The creature had thick black, leathery skin, a beak full of sharp teeth, long talons for feet, and membrane-like wings that spanned 10 feet, 7 inches, by their measure. You guessed it, a dragon had been trapped for some time before the eventual release.

New Guinea Dragon-Known as Ropen, its name means "demon flyer", it is an extremely pterosaur-like animal reported from islands just off of Papua New Guinea. Reported to be a large, frightening creature which scavenges for a living like a massive vulture, it is said that they spend the day in sea caves, then at dusk fly across the sea to the mainland or the islands. When they leave the caves, they allegedly have a bright green glow. Not much else is known.

Ethiopia Dragon- The Greek philosopher Aristotle reported that flying serpents were commonly seen in Ethiopia. That being said, they must have moved because now Zambia is the capitol of Dragons in Africa.

New Guinea Pterodactyl-ccording to a report in Papua New Guinea's The Independent newspaper, a 'dinosaur-like reptile' was seen on two occasions in the Lake Murray area, in Western Province.

Nambian Pterodactyl-In the late 1980s, noted cryptozoologist Roy Mackal led an expedition into Namibia from which he had heard reports of a prehistoric-looking creature with a wingspan of up to 30 feet.

Kongamato Dragon-The Kongamato is a reported pterosaur-like monster from the border area of Zambia, Angola and Congo. Similar to the extinct Rhamphorhynchus, it was reported in 1923. It was described as living along certain rivers, and very dangerous, often attacking small boats. It was red, with a wingspan of 4 to 7 feet. Members of the local Kaonde tribe identified it The natives, who were occasionally tormented by these creatures, described them as being featherless with smooth skin, having a beak full of teeth and a wingspan of between four and seven feet. When shown illustrations of pterosaurs, Melland reported, "every native present immediately and unhesitatingly picked out and identified it as a *kongamato*."In 1925, a native man was allegedly attacked by a creature that he identified as a pterosaur. This occurred near a swamp in Zambia where the man suffered a large wound in his chest that he said was caused by the monster's long beak. In 1932 an Englishman was attached by the same bat like monster. In 1956 the monster was seen on Lake Bangweulu in Northern Zambia. Two creatures were flying together. Wingspan was estimated to be about 3 1/2 feet and a beak-to-tail length of about 4 1/2 feet. In 1957, a patient came into a hospital with a severe wound in his chest by this monster. In 1988 in Namibia there were reports of a similar creature with a wingspan of up to **30 feet**. [See below left]

Arizona Dragon- When we go over to the United States, it gets even more interesting. A smaller pterosaur-like monster is known to residents who live on the desert fringes in Arizona. They have only heard it and seen shadows, but they certainly believe the animal is not normal.

Arizona Dragon- To make some of the stories more belivable, how about dead ones!! In Arizona, one of the monsterous Pterodactyl Dragons was killed as shown above right.

Texas Dragon- This picture following is believed to show the results of a pterodactyl Dragon hunt in Texas. There can be little doubt that large dragon-like monsters were still around in recent times and they may still be flying around out there.

Harlingen, Texas Monster – In 1976, Jackie Davis and Tracey Lawson reported seeing a "bird" on the ground that stood five feet tall, was dark in color with a bald head and a face like a gorilla's with a sharp, six-inch-long beak. Their parents uncovered tracks that had three toes and were eight inches across.

San Antonio, Texas Monster – In 1976, three elementary school teachers saw what they described as a pterodactyl swooping low over their cars as they drove. They said its wingspan was between 15 to 20 feet. One of the teachers commented that it glided through the air on huge, bony wings - like a bat's.

Los Fresnos, Texas Monster – In 1982 an ambulance driver was stopped while driving on Highway 100 but stopped when he saw a "large birdlike object" flying low over the area. He described it as black or grayish with a rough texture, but no feathers. It had a five- to six-foot wingspan, a hump on the back of its head, and almost no neck at all.

New York Monster – In 1961, a businessman flying his private plane over the Hudson River Valley claimed that he was "buzzed" by a large flying creature that he said "looked more like a pterodactyl out of the prehistoric ages."

California Monster –In the 1960s a couple driving through Trinity National Forest reported seeing the silhouette of a giant "bird" that they estimated to have a wingspan of 14 feet. They later described it as resembling a pterodactyl.

Another Texas Dragon-In Texas, A Flying lizard Dragon was shot down. [See below left]

Native American Dragon- The legend of the Thunderbird reaches back hundreds of years as part of the mythology of several Native American tribes of the western United States. According to the Native American myths, the giant Thunderbird could shoot lightning from its eyes and its wings were so enormous that they created peals of thunder when they flapped. There can be little doubt that this massive, flying monster was still around for millions of years. [See above right]

Utah Dragon- If pterosaurs really died out with the dinosaurs, then a depiction of one could not possibly exist in an ancient rock carving. Yet a pictograph found high on a cliff face near Thompson, Utah seems to show one of the flying reptiles plainly. This one was also called the thunderbird, but we can simply call it a dragon.

Panama Pterodactyl-On December 11, 1999, villagers travelling in a canoe reported seeing the creature wading in shallow water near Boboa. The following day, a Seventh Day Adventist pastor and a church elder say they saw the animal not far from the first sighting. The creature was described as having a body 'as long as a dump truck' and nearly two meters wide, with a long neck and a long slender tail. It was walking on two hind legs 'as thick as coconut palm tree trunks', and had two smaller forelegs. The head was similar in shape to a cow's head, with large eyes and 'sharp teeth as long as fingers.' The skin was likened to that of a crocodile, and the creature had 'largish triangular scoops on the back.' Additional images are shown below left.

Cuban Dragon-U. S. Marine Eskin C. Kuhn observed the two flying creatures shown next at Guantanamo Bay, Cuba in 1971. An Army soldier saw another giant "pterodactyl," that year, in Cuba as well. All three flying creatures had long tails. All three had prominent head crests. None of the three were like any bird or bat. [See drawinf above right]

Ohio Kraken-The United States Fish and Wildlife Service (FWS) recently released an image of a Pterodactyl hovering over the Hackensack River just south of Foshini Park. [Shown Below]

According to government sources, the image was taken by FWS scientists who were sent to investigate multiple sightings of the creature over the last year or so. Here is a pterosaur sighting received recently from an eye witness named Mark:

"It was around 9am on a Sunday morning in Oct. of 2005. I was in Mount Vernon, Ohio. I was coming to preach at a church out in the country (the same church I will soon be the church plant pastor of). This had been my first visit there to preach. There were many times in the trip that I slowed down because I wasn't sure I was still on the correct road or didn't want to pass the church (i.e., blink and you miss it). At one of those times I happen to notice a creature in the sky. Having no one behind me I took a moment to slow the car down and take a look at it. To my estimation it appeared to have no feathers. It was a leathery grayish color. The beak seemed to protrude from its face not like a separate part of the head, but looking to be the same color, etc. It's wings did not look like bird wings, but also appeared leathery and bat-like (I have seen actual bats in caves and zoos). The kicker, for me, was the tail: longer than most bird tails I am used to, no feathers, and with a diamond-shaped point at the end. I know how people can have a stigma about persons who have stories like mine, so I have been careful not to tell many people. I also have made it a point to look at the birds in Mount Vernon, Ohio. They are larger--many of the them--than in the lower central and southern areas of Ohio where I lived before, or grew up. However, all of the others birds I have seen have clearly had feathers on the body, wings, and tails, with beaks that look different from the rest of their facial make up (and certainly none with a diamond-shape point at the end of a long tail or bat-like wings). I am not very good at judging the size of animals in the air. I will say this, he was high up and yet I could tell everything about him/her that I told you. Easily larger than a bald eagle. "

Oregon Sighting- Here is another eye witness account. *"My name is Phillip O'Donnell. We live in Oregon. I really enjoy this website. The info about living dinosaurs is great! I just thought that you might like to know that in 2003 my brother and I saw a strange bird. It was perched in a tree for about 1 minute. It was about three feet tall with a white chest and black spots. I looked at through the binoculars and so did my brother. It had a horn-like thing protruding out of the back of its head that was pointing upwards and was not like a heron's tuff of hair. As it flew* *away we guessed the wingspan to be about 9 feet. I have seen many Great Blue Herons and I enjoy to watch them, but this bird was different. The wings were long and pointy. It returned the next year and we saw it in the same field. The sighting only lasted about 5 seconds. We briefly saw a long and very large pair of wings that had red streaks on them. They were also very bright like a mirror reflecting on sunlight. I have recently talked on the phone with Charlie Knight in Washington. He said that when he was a boy, he saw two pterosaurs that had a horn on back of their head. "* Sketch of the sighting is shown below left.

From "Dinosaurs by Design" by Dr. Duane Gish

Arizona Sighting- There is another account of a living Pterosaur from April of 1890. This time the eyewitness were two men riding horses across the hot Arizona desert near Tombstone. They noticed a large flying reptile with a six foot wing span and long slender body. As it was about to land the men shot and killed the creature. Knowing this was a significant find, the men are said to have cut off part of the wing and brought it back to town with them. A graphic from "Dinosaurs by Design" is shown above right.

Modern Ape Monster

That sort of brings us to big foot, yeti, ape-man just like the ape-men depicted 3000 years ago. Around the world these stupid foot prints keep showing up along with the occasional sighting of what looks to be a gigantic ape like biped.

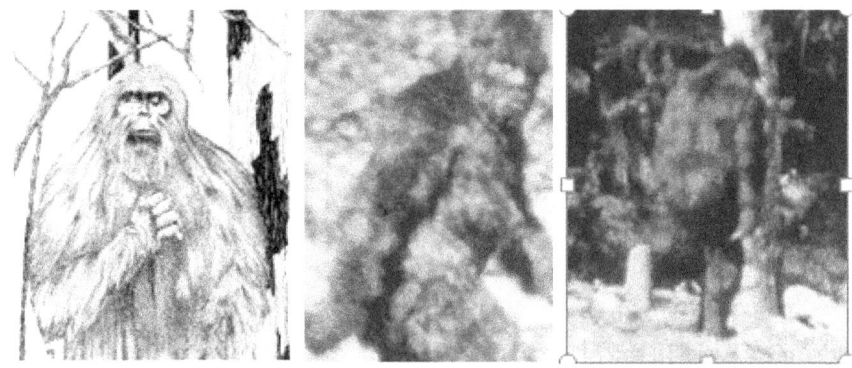

All over the United States, Canada, and many other parts of the world the same apelike things has been spotted and tracked even the skullcap of one from the Himalayas is now being protected by Buddhist monks. It would be difficult to say these guys don' exist especially with the Gigantopithecus [Giant Ape-man] remains are all over the place. It simply means that the geneticists of very ancient times survived the flood to reestablish the breed after the Pleistocene Extinction 10 thousand years ago. On the following page are just a few of the dozens and dozens of these massive footprints that are becoming more prevalent every year. Wait a minute! The yeti and big foot aren't 10 foot tall; they must be an offshoot of the Meganthropus or even the ape-men noted in drawings and images around the world from 3000 years ago when they were part of society..

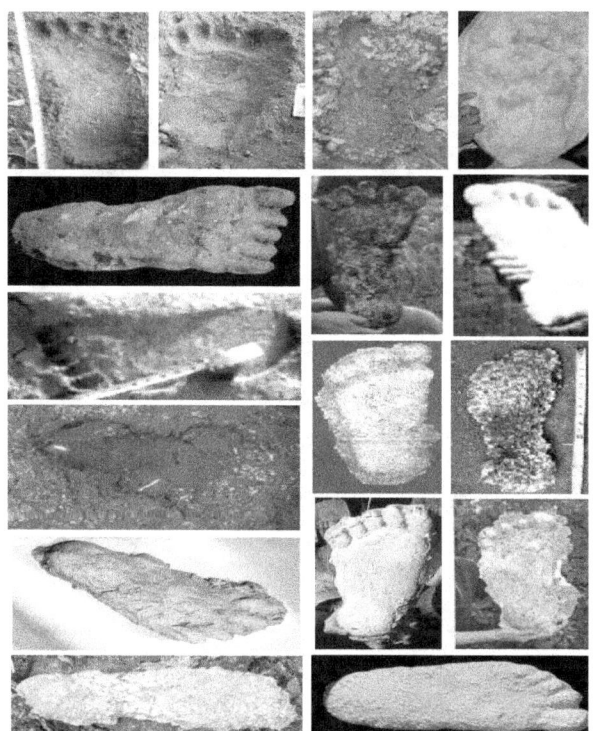

Sasquatch Ape Monster-This hominid is found all over the Pacific North West of the United States. It is undoubtedly the most famous mammal monster. We have taken many pictures, video, and casts of his large footprints. Primarily vegetarian, he has instinctive fear of humans. Occasionally this monster is aggressive. Their big footprints have been collected for many years. Here is a collection by one man in the Unites States.

If your very lucky, you get a glimpse of this monster throwback of the Babel Wars. Here is a sampling of some of the more famous sightings.

119

Manaha Ape Monster-This Hominid is found in the Great Lakes region of the United States. It is also known as windigo, eastern bigfoot or Ohio's Abombidible Snowman. Unlike the sasquatch this monster has a long "mane" of hair on the head and it is believed to be carnivorous. One individual in Missouri, took up residence near a town and tried to abduct pets and small children for a time.

Toonijuk Ape Monster-Found in Arctic Canada and Alaska, this one differs from Sasquatch by being huge. They are very human-like and are covered in long flowing hair as opposed to thick short hair. In Alaska the same kind of monster is called Arulataq.

Provo, Utah sighting- This apeman was filmed going through the brush as shown.

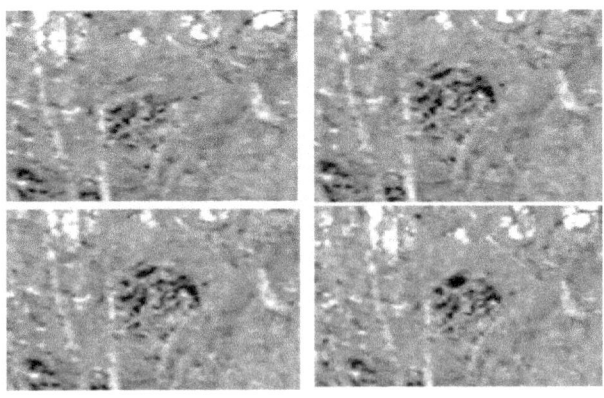

Oregon Apeman- In Oregon, in 2012 a similar apeman was spotted running to get away from the investigators.

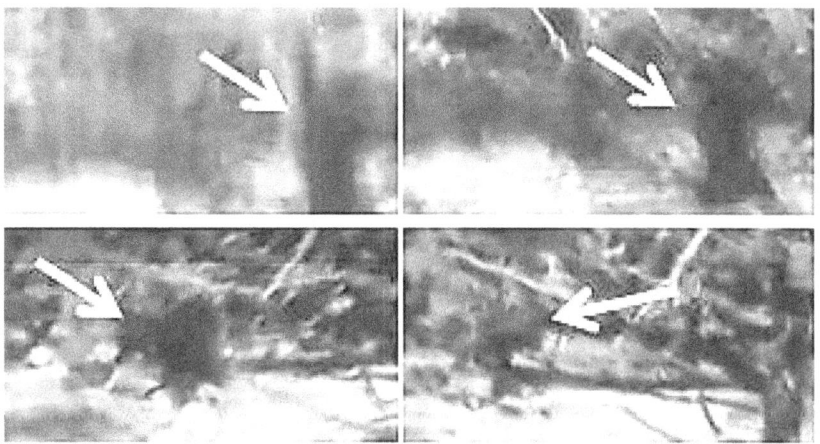

Sept 2012 Christmas Valley Oregon

Kentucky Apeman- As shown below left, a similar apeman was spotted in Jefferson county in 2009.

Washington Apeman- An almost identical sighting in Washington shows the Sasquatch running away from the scary people. [Below Right]

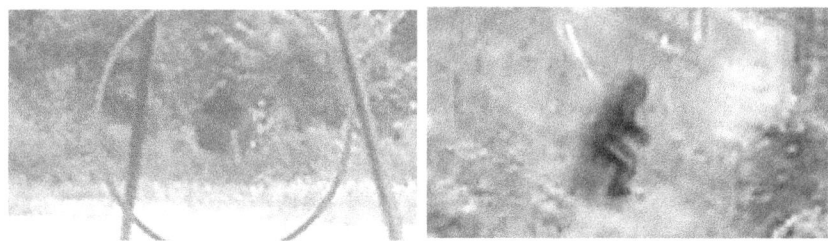

Jefferson County, Kentucky September 2009   Washington State

Wood Devil Ape Monster-Wood devils are found in Eastern United States. Supposedly they are tall and skinny. These monsters are considered hostile by the locals and are much feared. If you are thinking these things are only seen in Montana, look again. The map following shows just some of the sightings around the country. There can be little doubt that the remnants of the people turned into ape-men after the Babel War are still around and abound in the United States.

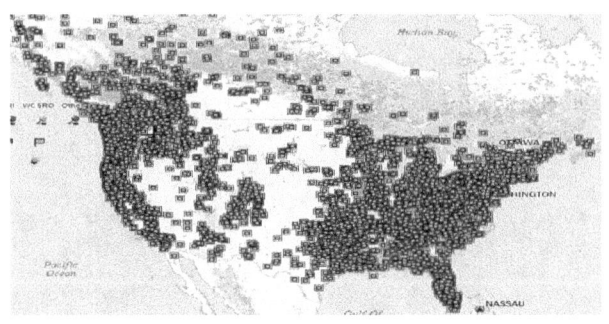 

Around the World we find these misshapen people. The images of these monsters after the Babel War were not simply figments of their imagination. The people were real and the images are still being witnessed today. Here is a sampling of other ape-men.

Sisemite Ape Monster-Sisemite is found in Central America. A medium sized, 5 foot tall humanoid, this guy is covered in black hair which grew almost to the ground. **DeLoys's Ape Monster-**DeLoys's Ape is found all over the Amazon River Valley. Also known as Mono Grande or didi, this guy almost looks like a giant spider monkey without a tail. It was named Ameranthropoids Loysi . Its picture is shown above right.

Ucu Ape Monster-Ucu is found in the Andes Mountains and is also known as ucumar or ukumar-zupia. Similar to the Sasquatch, many sightings have occurred over the years. It is said to be fond of the Payo plant.

Long Hair Ape Monster- African long haired Ape has been found all over the African continent. About the same size as a man, they have long hair on their bodies of a reddish or brownish color, and are man-like, somewhat similar to Sasquatch.

Giant African Ape Monster-Giant African hominoids have been spotted in Sudan, Kenya, Zaire and Cameroons. These huge humanoids get to be nearly 14 feet tall.

Fating'ho Ape Monster-Fating'ho have been sighted in Senegal Africa. The thing that is most known is that it is a large bipedal primate of some kind. This thing is also known as the Wokolo.

European Wildmen Monsters-European wildmen have been spotted in Eastern Europe. Reportedly that are wild humanoids that don't belong to our species. They are described as being covered in hair except for their faces, the palms of their hands, soles of their feet and their knees. Their hair is coarse hair rather than fur. Similar to Neanderthal, they do not have any society and have not been reported in recent times, so many believe them to be extinct.

Fear Liath Mor Monsters-Fear Liath Mor were spotted in Northern Scotland. These creatures are said to be large, grey colored, and fearsome-looking. Unlike Sasquatch, these monsters stalk people who trespass in their territory.

Running Man Monster-The "Running man" was spotted in Scotland and is almost identical to sasquatch. One sighting describes a creature whose face was almost human and it was running all the time. It has been known to run alongside cars to look inside the windows.

Basajaun Monster-Basajaun is found in Spain. This creature is known as a "hairy giant" and he is extremely hostile towards humans. Even so, he visits homes looking for food. In one recorded attack occurred when a group of paleontologists was attacked by two of the creatures. They are about 5 or 6 feet tall.

Ventimiglian Giant-The Ventimiglian giant is found in Northern Italy. There have been many sighting of this monster, especially recently. Very similar to Sasquatch, they are described as hairy human-like giants over 7 feet tall. One sighting detailed three of the creatures milling around together in a forest. They had extremely short thick necks.

Scandinavian "Bigfoot"-Scandinavian "bigfoot" was sighted in Swedenand Norway. A number of people have encountered this large, long-haired hominid, similar to the Arulataq or Sasquatch of the United States.

Vedi-Vedi have been spotted in Croacia and Hungary. This hairy Wildman has been sighted for many years. Many cases involve females sneaking in to stables where the male farm-hands have been sleeping, then cozying up beside them. I'm not going to say any more about this one except it is similar to Sasquatch which may give the sasquatch hunters another thing to worry about.

Alma- Alma have been spotted all over Western Russia. Reportecly, they are wild humanoids that are spoken of as "retarded Neanderthal men". They are Neanderthal-like except they seem incapable of most reasoning and communicate with loud "BOOM" noises.

Kaptar- Kaptar have been seen [and even more] in Mongolia and Russia. Similar to Neanderthals they, reportedly, trade and even interbreed with the Mongolians and Siberians. Offspring are ugly but are extremely gifted mentally. No telling what the Vedi and Kaptar would do if they were introduced.

Baramanu-Baramanu, or "Big Hairy One" has been seen in Pakistan. It is reported to resemble prehistoric man and many footprints have been found of the somewhat prehistoric man monster. An expedition unsuccessfully tried to find one of these guys in 1990.

Yeren- This monster is from China. Sometimes known as the Chinese "wildman", the yeren is more apelike than sasquatch ape-like, and covered in long hair. Several have been killed, but the corpses were never examined, [possibly eaten].

Malaysian "bigfoot"- This monster was seen on the Maylay peninsula. This is a sasquatch-like creature that only has four toes. Is much feared by the locals.

Hibagon- This monster is found in Japan. The Japanese version of the sasquatch.

Kapre- This monster was spotted in the Philippines. He is a tall, sasquatch-like creature from several of the Philippine islands. It is usually regarded as a harmless inhabitant.

Solomon "sasquatch"-Generally identical to sasquatch, this one is found on Solomon islands. A tall, hairy hominoid.

Bipedal Land Monsters

Possibly called Behemoth in the Bible, could these monsters have survived the Babel Wars? I think the answer is that they did. While the monsters were made to be smaller than those before the Heaven War there can be little doubt that the DNA structures of these animals were similar.

Texas Bipedal Monster- Sometimes called Mountain boomer, A 6 foot tall dinosaur-like animal reported from areas of western Texas. If it exists, think it is some kind of large, bipedal lizard. A boy claimed to have watched a greenish colored lizard with black markings and a yellow-orange belly running on its hind legs away from him. A second witness took a series of pictures, but they are indistinct. Later, there is one very good picture, showing a man holding up a 3 foot long lizard with small front legs and long, strong hind Legs that resembles what was reported earlier.

Similar African Image- While that one is not available, the one below shows a smaller version of the bipedal dinosaurs captured on film from somewhere in Africa. In this image, the monster has taken down a rhinoceros or found a dead one to eat. The story goes like this. In 1932 John Johnson , a Swedish plantation owner, was traveling with a servant in the Kasai valley, in the Belgian Congo. They encountered a Rhinoceros, and, while attempting to pass it without detection, were surprised by a large creature rushing out of the undergrowth and attacking the rhinoceros. The servant ran away and Johnson fainted. He awoke to see that the creature was eating the rhinoceros. *"It was reddish in color, with blackish-colored stripes,"* he said later. *"It had a long snout and numerous teeth."* He decided that the creature, over 40 feet long, was a Tyrannosaurus or a descendent. He also said "The legs were thick; it reminded me of a lion, built for speed". [See next right]

Jewish Bipedal Monster- In the Jewish Synagogue Umm El-Kanatir we find art from 400 to 700 A.D. showing one of these monsters Notice that the feet on this monster had three toes exactly like earlier dinosaurs.[Above right]

Vancouver Bipedal Monster-There are 2 reports of the Vancouver Island bipedal lizard; one from Vancouver Island, and a report of the exact same creature from Texada Island. Both areas are heavily forested, but very remote.

Western North American Monster- The Anasazi dinosaur shown on the pottery shows that these things were in the U.S.A. not too long ago. [Below Left]

Chinese Bipedal Monster- Holy Men from the Ming Dynasty [1368 – 1644 B.C.] shows one of the bipedal monsters that were seen or remembered. [Below right]

126

Chinese Bipedal Monster- As shown below, the Chinese were well aware of these monsters in the not too distant past as the image shows.

Scandinavian Two legged Behemoth-Scandinavian countries had about as many tales of dragons as anywhere in the world.[1] One old legend describes a reptile-like animal that had a body about the size of a large cow. Its two back legs were long and strong. But its front legs were remarkably short. And its jaws were quite large. One of the unique things about many dinosaurs was their short front legs, compared to their long, strong back legs. Many also had large jaws. Examples of dinosaurs which fit are the Edmontosaurus or Iguanodon-like.

Four Legged Monster

The Acambaro Dinosaurs- Waldemar Julsrud, a German hardware merchant in Acambaro, Mexico, was riding his horse on the lower slope of El Toro Mountain on a sunny morning in 1944 when he spotted some partially exposed hewn stones and a ceramic object half buried in the dirt. Among the thousands of artifacts excavated were items that turned Julsrud's mansion into "the museum that scared scientists." Sculpted in various colors of clay were figurines of dinosaurs. Dr. Ivan T. Sanderson was amazed in 1955 to find that there was an accurate representation of the American dinosaur Brachiosaurus, almost totally unknown at that time to the general public.

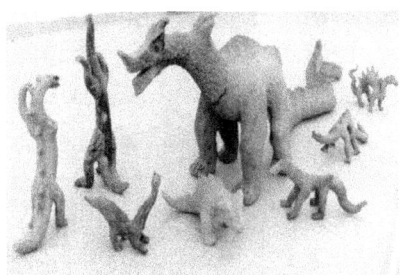 

Mayan Monsters- There can be little doubt that the ICA stone engravings show dinosaur-like monsters that roamed South and Central America in the not too distant past..

Nguma-Monene -This is Mackal's depiction of the *Nguma-Monene [below]*. Under the name of *Badigui*, it was one of the basic catecories of reports which Heuvelmans counted the same as the *Mokele-Mbembe* and suggested could be a surviving dinosaur

Aseka-moke, **Njago-gunda**, **Ngamba-namae**, **Chipekwe** or **Irizima** in another language is an elephant-sized monster that lives in the Congo and possibly Cameroon. It has one horn and its name means "Elephant Killer" It is very ferocious and will kill anything that gets in its way. It seems to resemble a ceratopsian, a type of dinosaur with horns as shown below left.

Mahamba as shown above right, is a monster rumored to lurk in the Democratic Republic of the Congo's Lake Likouala around the swamp region. It is purported to be an enormous crocodile, reaching lengths of up to 50 feet. Some have speculated that it is a freshwater relic of the mosasaurs with legs. The Bobangi aboriginals have proclaimed this animal to be unlike any other they have seen.

Colorado Monster- Huge granite carvings of the time show dinosaur-like monsters still roaming around. Quickly sketched so as not to be eaten. Looks like the thing was a little larger than the rhinoceros depicted so we can see it was not as large as the former beasts. [See below left]

DRAGON FIGURE
CHINA. 25-221 A.D.

Chinese 4 footed Monster- If we move to the far east, we find the same type of monster in the not too distant past. The figure above right shows one of the non-flying dragons, described in china around the first century AD,

Carlisle Cathedral Monster- Engravings in the floor of Carlisle Cathedral appear to be of dinosaurs. They are on the tomb of bishop Richard Bell, who died in 1496. The question is why are these brass engravings here? If they are not dinosaurs why do they have such long necks that they use to wrap around each other? The bishops tomb is engraved with things that he enjoyed such as hunting and foliage and these dinosaur engravings...

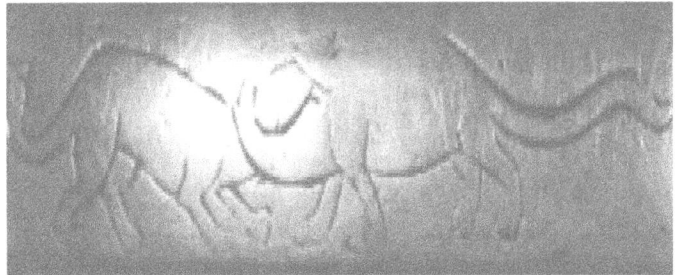

Babylon Quadraped -One "behemoth" story from the ancient land of Sumer in Babylon tells of the hero Gilgamesh. He decided to make a name for himself by traveling to a distant land to cut great cedar trees needed for his city. He reached the forest with fifty volunteers and discovered a huge reptile-like animal which ate trees and reeds. The story simply says that Gilgamesh killed it and cut off its head for a trophy.[1]

Irelandish Quadraped Monster-Around 900AD, an Irish writer recorded an encounter with a large beast with "iron" spikes on its tail which pointed backwards. Its head was shaped a little like a horse's. And it had thick legs with strong claws. These details match features of dinosaurs like the *Kentrosaurus* or *Stegosaurus*. They had sharp-pointed spines on their tails, thick legs, strong claws and long skulls.

French Quadraped Behemoth-The city of Nerluc in France was renamed in honor of the killing of a "dragon" there. This animal was bigger than an ox and had long, sharp, pointed horns on its head.

Peruvian Behemoth- On a rock cliff in Peru we find that these monsters were hunted by the ancient Peruvians. [Below left]

St. George Monster-Many items show how St. George killed one of these monstrous dinosaurs a number of years ago. A wonderful medieval depiction is seen at the Palau de La Generalitat in Barcelona Spain. St. George's Chapel contains an altar cloth illustrating St. George's slaying of a dragon. [Above right]

French Chateaus Monsters- Built in the early 1500's a number of re-created dinosaurs have been depicted on wall s of Chateaus including Château Azay-le-Rideau and Château de Blois. The depictions are shown below, but they certainly look like dinosaurs before anyone had ever coined the name. There is no telling how many of these things were seen or fought against.

In Rome there is a similar image outside at the Church of St. Louis. This served as the national church was completed in the 1580's. There can be little mistake that a number of people saw and described these things in extreme detail.

Egyptian Dinosaurs

Everyone has seen the dinosaurs from the tablet of Narmer, the first unifying King of Egypt. If not, it is shown next left along with the blow up drawing.

Sumerian Duplicate

Some may not know how very close Sumeria and Egypt was during the time of the Bharata War, but, the dinosaur images above right are from Sumeria and an almost identical match even to the crossing of the necks. The question might what places did not see these things? Let's travel to Bolivia and see if more recent finds have come about.

Bolivian Monster

In 1883 "Scientific American" had a story about "A Bolivian Saurian" which adds credibility to this sighting. According to the story, this massive beast was shot. That didn't do the trick so it was finally hit by 36 balls before dying. The Brazilian Minister at La Paz, Bolivia, had remitted to the Minister of Foreign Affairs in Rio photographs of drawings of this extraordinary saurian killed on the Beni. The body was then and sent to La Paz." The "monster" was reported to be almost 40 feet long from snout to point of the tail, which latter was flattened. It's head resemblance the head of a dog and its legs were short, ending with formidable claws. The legs and abdomen sported a kind of scale armor, and all the back is protected by a still thicker and double plates, starting from behind the ears of the anterior head, and continuing to the tail. The neck was long, and the belly large such that it almost dragged the ground. It must have looked like a massive crocodilian monster, but the drawings seem to have been lost, so we can't see the beast.

Fawcett Monster-Explorer Percy Fawcett mentioned dinosaur-like animals briefly on several occasions as occurring in the Río Guaporé area on the border of Bolivia and Brazil. In the Madidi region of La Paz Department in northwestern Bolivia, and in swamps around the Rio Acre in Acre State, Brazil. Percy H. Fawcett, Exploration Fawcett (London: Hutchinson, 1955).

Clark Monster-Leonard Clark heard rumors of an animal resembling a sauropod dinosaur from Peruvian Indians around the Río Marañón, Peru, in 1946. He wrote about these stories in a book in 1953.

Basto Monster- In 1975, a Swiss businessman hired a seventy five- year-old guide named Sebastian Bastos, who told him that the Amazonian Indians knew of animals 18 feet long that overturn canoes and kill humans. Bastos himself had survived an attack several years earlier. Be careful if you go to Bolivia.

134

Mokele-mbembe Monster

By far the most talked about discovery of a 4 legged dinosaur monster would be the Mokele-mbembe. As depicted below.

There is a swamp in Africa that is bigger than Minnesota. Only 20% has been explored. The natives to that area claim there is a long necked monster that's description is very much like a dinosaur. Some guys went to explore it but they said mosquitoes landed on them hourly by the 1000s. The Bible talks about "Behemoth" in the book of Job and says that this beast lives in swamps. The description of this beast is the same as a dinosaur although some have tried to explain it away as a hippo or elephant which does not work because Behemoth's tail is described as a cedar rather than a puny stick. Whether the Bohemeth Job talked about had 2 walking legs or 4, is not known, but this certainly is a nasty monster and exhibitions since 1909 have been on going to get evidence in one of the most inhospitable places in the world.

AMERICAN EXPEDITION 1909 -Naturalist Carl Hagenbeck recounted in his autobiography how two separate individuals - a German named Hans Schomburgh and an English hunter - told him about a **"huge monster, half elephant, half dragon,"** which lived in the Congo swamps. Later, another naturalist, Joseph Menges, related to Hagenbeck that "some kind of dinosaur, seemingly akin to the brontosaurs," inhabited the swamps. Hagenbeck soon sent an expedition to the Congo to search for the monster, but the effort was quickly aborted due to disease and hostile natives.

GERMAN EXPEDITION 1913--In 1913, Capt. Freiherr von Stein zu Lausnitz was sent by the German government to explore the Cameroon. Von Stein wrote of a unique animal called, in the local tongue, Mokele-mbembe, said to inhabit the areas near the Ubangi, Sangha, and Ikelemba Rivers. Von Stein described the creature thus:

"The animal is said to be of a brownish-gray color with a smooth skin, its size approximately that of an elephant; at least that of a hippopotamus. It is said to have a long and very flexible neck and only one tooth, but a very long one; some say it is a horn. A few spoke about a long muscular tail like that of an alligator. It is said to climb the shore even at daytime in search of food; its diet is said to be entirely vegetable. At the Ssombo River I was shown a path said to have been made by this animal in order to get at its food. The path was fresh and there were plants of the described type [a liana] nearby"

AMERICAN EXPEDITION 1920- A 32-men-strong expedition was sent out from the Smithsonian Institution in Washington D.C. After six days, African guides found large, unexplained tracks along the bank of a river and later the team heard mysterious "roars, which had no resemblance with any known animal," coming from an unexplored swamp. However, the Smithsonian's hunt for Moklele-Mbembe was to end in tragedy. During a train-ride through a flooded area where an entire tribe was said to have seen the dinosaur, the locomotive suddenly derailed and turned over. Four team members were crushed to death under the cars and another half dozen seriously injured.

AMERICAN EXPEDITION 1932-In 1932, American cryptozoologist Ivan Sanderson was traveling in Africa and came across large hippo-like tracks in a region with no hippos. He was told by the natives that they were made by a creature named the "Mgbulu-e M'bembe." Later, Sanderson saw something in the water that seemed too large to be a hippo, but it disappeared before he could investigate further.

AMERICAN EXPEDITION 1972-In 1960, herpetologist James H. Powell, Jr. took interest in the African dragons and organized an expedition to the Congo in 1972. Powell's expedition, unfortunately, was fraught with problems (the United States and the Congo had poor relations at the time). Many months of hardships such as snake-bites, near-drownings and tropical diseases only led to more witness testimonies about Mokele-Membe and another lizard-like creature which locally was called "n'yamala."

AMERICAN EXPEDITION 1976-In 1976, James Powell decided to go to Gabon instead, inspired by a book called "Trader Horn." (In 1927, the book, a memoir of the author's time in Gabon, specifically along the Ogooue River, was written by Englishman Alfred Aloysius Smith. He recorded hearing of a creature called the "jago-nini" and identified it with the "amali," a creature whose tracks he had seen). He was quick to realize they were probably identical to the Mokele-mbembe. Furthermore, Powell heard local legends of the n'yamala, and locals identified pictures of a sauropod dinosaur as bearing the most resemblance to the animal.

GERMAN EXPEDITION 1980-An expedition mounted by engineer Herman Regusters and his wife Kia managed to make its way to Lake Tele, where they heard the growls and roars of an unknown creature. They also claimed to have photographed Mokele-Mbembe in the lake, as well as watching it walk on land through the brush. According to Regusters, the creature they saw was 30-35 feet long.

AMERICAN EXPEDITION 1980-Powell launched another expedition in 1980, but this time cryptozoologist Roy P. Mackal came along. Powell and Mackal found that a large number of reports came from the banks of the Likouala-aux-herbes River near Lake Tele. They said that most witnesses maintained that the animal was between 15-30 feet long (a long neck accounted for much of the length). The creature was also said to be a rust color, and that some had been seen to possess a frill or crest.

AMERICAN EXPEDITION 1981-Yet another expedition was organized in 1981 - this time composed of Mackal, J. Richard Greenwell, M. Justin Wilkinson, and Congolese zoologist Marcellin Agnagna. The expedition encountered what they believed was a Congo "dinosaur" along the Likouala River, when they heard a large animal leaping into the water near Epena. They also discovered a path of broken branches supposedly made by the animal, as well as a number of footprints.

AFRICAN EXPEDITION 1983-In April, 1983, a Congolese expedition led by Marcellin Agnagna, a zoologist from the Brazzaville Zoo, arrived to Lake Tele. Agnagna claimed to have seen the beast some 275 meters out in the lake. The animal held its thin, reddish head - which had crocodile-looking, oval eyes and a thin nose - on a height of 90 cm and looked from side to side, almost as if it was watching him. According to Agnagna, the animal was a reptile, though not a crocodile, nor a python or a freshwater turtle.

BRITISH EXPEDITION 1985-86-Englishman William J. Gibbons (presently living in Canada) talked to several eye-witnesses who gave him valuable information about the Mokele-Mbembe. He is currently convinced that the dinosaur exists, but at the time was unable to prove it.

JAPANESE EXPEDITION 1987-A piece of blurry video footage filmed by a Japanese film crew supposedly showing the creature in Lake Tele remains disputable evidence of the animal's existence. The film is indistinct and grainy, possibly just showing two men in a boat with one of them standing upright in the front of the vessel, as is common in Africa.

BRITISH EXPEDITION 1990-Author and explorer Redmond O'Hanlon returned from his failed expedition convinced that witnesses must have mistaken wild elephants, crossing rivers with their trunk in the air, for a prehistoric Mokele-Mbembe.

BRITISH EXPEDITION 1992-William Gibbons tried again six years later, this time together with American explorer Rory Nugent. Together they searched almost two thirds of the unexplored Bai River while also examining two small lakes North West of Lake Tele. These are Lake Fouloukuo and Lake Tibeke, which are surprisingly absent from most maps. Both are said to be haunts of Mokele-Mbembe. Rory Nugent also took two interesting photographs of something most unusual in Lake Tele. One is said to possibly be the head of a Mokele Mbembe. Below is the blurry photo and a drawing of same.

A second, video shows something moving extremely fast across the lake as shown below.

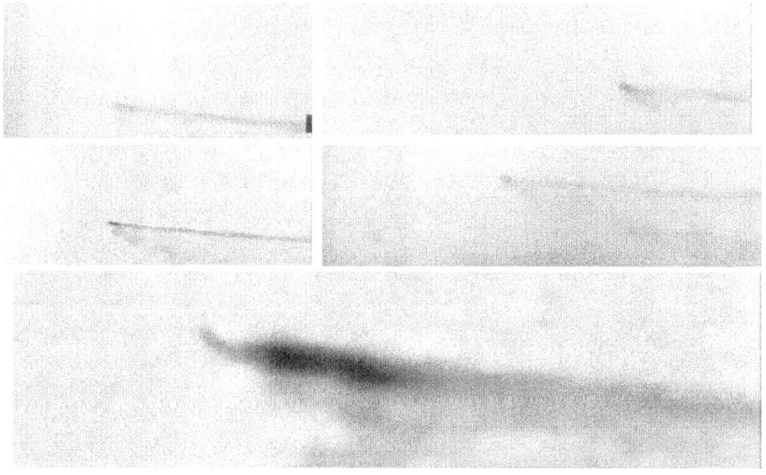

Some say this is the most popular of the "living dinosaurs". In popular opinion, it is thought to be a modern species of Atlantosaurus, or perhaps a very small descendent of the Titanosaurs. A sketch of this thing is shown below left.

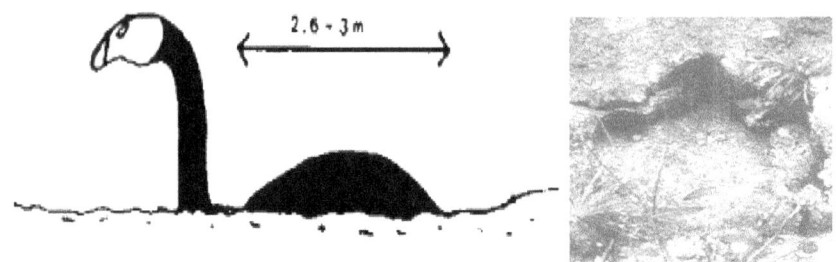

Fresh Dinosaur Footprints in the mud- Dr. Roy Mackal was not very successful bringing back one of the behemoths or Dragons of Africa, but he did provide some level of proof. He and his team found a very clear footprint in the dirt in the same area as a sighting. The footprint had been made by a 4 footed monster creature. It was no more than 1-day old at the time a photo was taken. It is definitely a three toed monster. [Above right]

Modern Sea Serpents

This group of monsters seem to be related to one of 3 prehistoric varieties including the Plesiosaur or Kronosaur as depicted first [4 flippered shorter tailed monster], Mosasaur or Basilosaur [depicted second- more aggressive meat eating best],   the Cadborosaur longer more placid beast that could display several humps on the water, and a long necked pinniped called **Megalotaria longicolli***e* which was a hairy variety similar to Cadborasaur [shown last].

I have tried to put these creatures to their closest relative, but many times all we see are bumps so, please excuse wrong . The first and largest group contains the Pinniped and Cadborosaurs.

Dead Cadborasaurs shown below

North American Sightings

Captured Sea Serpent- the diagram below shows a baby sea serpent released after capture. There is little mistake that this was a Cadborasaur type.

Captain Hagelund's 'baby *Cadborosaurus*'
Captured in 1968 but released out of pity

British Columbia Sea Serpent -The sea serpent shown below was found in British Columia and described as being 30 foot long, having hide like sandpaper, the head of a horse, and spinelike quils. The monster had been dead for about 2 months when this picture was taken.

British Columbia Sighting- The Cadborosaurus below was spotted off the coast of British Colombia recently. The undulating humps are the big give away.

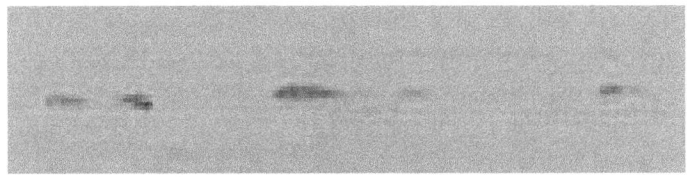

Lake Memphremagog Sea Serpent-Memphre is the most famous of the Quebec lake monsters, this creature has had various descriptions given to it. All modern reports speak of an immense serpentine beast similar to the Lake Champlain Sea Serpent.

Baltimore Monster- The picture below shows an 1879 image of what appears to be a sea serpent.

43. The *City of Baltimore* sea-serpent, 1870

Cadborosaurus willsi- This one, nicknamed **Caddy**, is living on the Pacific Coast of North America. There have been more than 300 claimed sightings during the past 200 years, in British Columbia and San Francisco Bay. To make it even more believable, a purported Cadborosaurus carcass was retrieved from the stomach of a sperm whale in Naden Harbor in 1937. It resembles a serpent with vertical coils or humps in tandem behind the horse-like head and long neck, with a pair of small elevating front flippers, and either a pair of hind flippers, or a pair of large webbed hind flippers fused to form a large fan-like tail region that provides powerful forward propulsion.

White River Sea Serpent -- White River monster has been spotted in Arkansas. Nicknamed "whitey", this creature only shows up for a couple weeks a year. It is said to be serpentine, with a spikey fin down it's back and a "horn" or bony projection out its snout. [Shown below left]

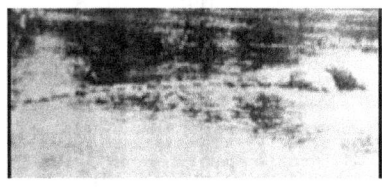 

Lake Memphremagog Sea Serpent-Shown to the right is photo evidence of the recent string of sightings of the Des Moines sea serpent that local fishermen have sought for decades.[Shown above right]

Pressie Sea Serpent Monster -Pressie, also known as South Bay Bessie, has been spotted in various Great Lakes. Reported for many years it is said to be a large, serpentine beast, that may behave like a porpoise. There is a photograph of one of the Lake Superior creatures and one of the creatures in Lake Michigan was allegedly killed, stuffed, and kept in a local museum. [Shown below left]

Lake Flathead Sea Serpent -The Flathead Lake monster is described as a very fast, grey-colored creature, rather similar to ogopogo. [Shown above right]

Massechusetts Serpent of 1639 -This is believed to be the first American sea serpent, reported from Cape Ann, Massachusetts, in 1639. [Shown below left]

 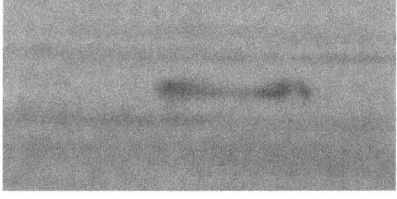

Manipogo -Lake monster in Lake Manitoba. Generally similar to other sea monsters, it is described as being 30 feet long and brown. [Shown above right]

Iliamna Lake Monster –Another Lake monster in southern Alaska.

Caddy -A large snakelike creature seen from the coast of Alaska to Oregon, Most sightings are close to Vancover Island .reports of the creature go back to pre-Columbian times, with some Indian petroglyphs seeming to depict the creature . [Left below]

Connecticut Sea Monsters- [Shown above right] There have numerous sightings of sea monsters back to 1638. In 1878 one was seen "It was seemingly not fifteen rods off. It was a horrible looking head, with a wide open month. The head disappeared and a portion of the body was shown, forming an arc under which it would have been easy to have driven a team of oxen. There were several smaller curves, indicating a long body." In 1886 there was another sighting of a 100 foot long monster with . a big black head and eyes as big as small plates. The head kept rising higher and higher until 10 feet of the neck appeared. Another encounter on a Yacht reported in 1881 indicating he raised his head and took survey of the surroundings. He was the color of gulf weed, mottled with black spots, and was about 40 feet long.

Oak-ness monster -The monster is about 8 feet long and it doesn't surface often. Recent photo taken of what is thought to be the Oak-ness monster of Lake Merritt show that it's black, it's big, it has spikes on its head , its tongue sticks out, and it's got typical round monster humps. [Below left]

Gloucester Sea Serpent – [As shown above right] In 1817, approximately three hundred reputable residents of coastal Massachusetts villages claimed to have seen a dark brown, smooth-skinned creature which moved by means of vertical undulations of its sixty foot long, serpentine body. The monster was named "Gloucester Sea Serpent," was seen continuously for 2 years then additional reports were made off New England and Canada as late as 1840.

Lake Erie "Bessie"-In **Lake Erie** we find the "South Bay Bessie". Since the 1960s it this creature has been seen many times by many people. The descriptions have it as a 30-50 long snake-like creature about as round as a bowling ball. The reported creature seems to appear when the water is calm.

Other Canadian Beasts-Two others include the New Brunswick Lake Utopia Monster and Manipogo of Lake Manitoba in **Canada.**

Louisiana's Sea Monster - The finny tribe killed this next one in 1856 off the coast of Louisiana. Length of the body from point of nose to the tip of the tail was 20 feet long and it was also 20 feet wide at the center, 7 feet wide head with a 3.5 foot mouth. The skin covered monster also had horns that were 3 foot long. When cut open, its liver was the size of a rice cask. The picture below left shows the monster.

Georgia's "Altamaha"-Georgia's version of the creature. Named after the river it frequents, the Altamaha, this mysterious creature is said to be large, dark, has two humps and churns the water in a strange way when surfacing or submerging. The local newspaper, The Darien News, has recorded a large number of sightings. Above right is a sketch by one of the witnesses.

Montana Monster-Another Plesiosaur like creature is called the Flathead Lake Monster in **Montana**
Caddy

Professor P. LeBlond of the University of British Columbia told a meeting of zoologists about the many sightings of 'Caddy'—short for Cadborosaurus—around the British Columbia coast and as far south as Oregon. The remains of a three-metre juvenile 'Caddy' have actually been found in the stomach of a whale. Photographs taken at the Naden Harbor whaling station at Queen Charlotte Islands show a well-preserved 10-foot baby Caddy taken from the stomach of a sperm whale that had recently swallowed it before the whale was killed by hunters. The authors interpret the creature in the photographs as a serpentine animal with the classic camel-like head and a tail region having two hind flippers.

In 1937 the Naden Harbor whaling station in the Queen Charlotte Islands was excited about the news that some fishermen had discovered a strange animal in the stomach of a recently harvested whale. The creature was about ten feet long and had odd characteristics such as a camel-like head, a long elongated body of serpentine proportions and curiously shaped fins above and a tail. The station manager, F. S. Huband, and G. V. Boorman, the acting medical officer, took photographs taken of the animal and sent tissue samples taken from the remains to the Fisheries station in Nanaimo and to the Provincial Museum in Victoria for analysis. Tragically, the tissue samples sent to Nanaimo vanished and the samples sent to Victoria were wrongly identified by curator Francis Kermode as belonging to a fetal baleen whale and no one knows what happened to them after Kermode examined them. So the only tangible proof of the existence of heretofore previously legendary animals was lost forever. However two sets of the photographs were discovered by Captain William Hagelund, who published a selection in his book "Whalers No More", and also by Paul LeBlond who included them in his book "Cadborosaurus: Survivor of the Deep".

Pensacola Florida Monster

Sometimes, people are the meal. Like many of the others, this is identified as an "Unknown Sea Creature". But the description and drawing of the sole survivor looked like a plesiosaur.

In Pensacola, Florida, 1962 five teenagers decided to go scuba diving off the coast about two miles there is an old sunken ship right off the harbor. Here is the story that Edward Brian McCleary wrote. He was the only survivor. Five teenagers went scuba diving out by this sunken ship in 1962. Edward (The sole survivor of a monster attack) lives in Jacksonville, He said the following:

" We were in an Air Force rescue raft bound for a sunken ship a few miles off the coast. Midway out, we were caught in a storm and dragged out to sea. When the storm cleared, we were in a dense fog....We began to hear strange noises, rather like the splashing of a porpoise... also a sickening odor like that of dead fish. The noise got closer to the raft and it was then we heard a loud hissing sound. Out in the fog we saw what looked like a long pole, about ten feet high, sticking straight up out of the water. On top was a bulb like structure." Like a light bulb? Round with a beak on it. "It bent in the middle and went under. It appeared several more times getting closer to the raft." "The silence was broken once again by something out of the fog. I can only describe it as a high-pitched whine. We panicked. All five of us put on our fins and went into the water.... 'Keep together and try for the ship,' I yelled. After we were in the water we became split up in the fog. From behind I could hear the screams of my comrades one by one. I got a closer look at the thing just before my last friend went under. The neck was about twelve feet long,

148

brownish- green and smooth looking. The head was like that of a sea-turtle except more elongated, with teeth. ....There appeared to be what looked like a dorsal fin when it dove under for the last time. Also, as best I am able to recall, the eyes were green with oval pupils." His four friends got eaten by it. He heard them screaming as they went under. He said, "I finally made it to the ship, the top of which protruded from the water, and stayed there for most of the night, early that morning I swam to shore and was found by the rescue unit."

Florida Sea Monster

A number of sightings of this monster has gotten people to talk. Some believe it to be some massive sea cow, but the long distance between the nose and back of the head have gotten people to wonder. Here are some of the snapshots from recent video taken of the beast.

White River Monster

And this account from Arkansas. Arkansas has its share of weird creatures lurking in forests and lakes . . . but enough about the Clinton family. Now, our journey takes us a little further north on Highway 67 to the small town of Newport Arkansas. This town has a version of the Loch Ness Monster which is widely accepted as being real by the townspeople. The White River Monster even has his own game preserve.

From about 1915 to the late 1970's, residents of Newport reported seeing a monster in the White River. This monster, nicknamed "Whitey", was described as being snake-like and at least thirty feet long. Witnesses reported that it made a loud bellowing noise and had a spiny backbone. Many reports were made by fisherman and campers along the river. In 1971, two men reported that they saw three-toed tracks along the muddy river banks and a places where the trees and vegetation had been broken because of the monster's size. The creature was even photographed in 1971 by Cloyce Warren of the White River Lumber Company.

Mexican Lake Monster

A young man from Mexico, Mr Hector Rivera, took the photo [above right] from a moving car on the 4th of September 2000, but the driver never stopped. Miss Tibbs, a local resident, also saw the thing from a different location. She indicated that she heard a *"thunderin' splash behind us. It was 'orrible it was, all green and filthy, rose like a giant, water everywhere, I feared for me life I did, thought I was a gonner. It must 'ave smelled the chicken wings.""*

Bear Lake Monster

In the upper northeastern corner of Utah is beautiful Bear Lake. Bear Lake is called home to a really, really, really big snake monster. Said to resemble a huge brown snakelike monster, nearly 90 feet long, a legend of this massive thing has been around from the days when only Indians inhabited this area. When white settlers came to the valley, the Shoshone Indians inhabiting the area told of how the creature had often captured and carried away their people. Their description of the animal sounded much like a large crocodile or even a dragon, but mostly it sounds like a massive serpent. According to the many who have spied the snake, it has a thin head, a large mouth, and **small legs** that it utilizes to move swiftly through the water. The slithering snake like-creature has also been described as spouting water upwards from its mouth and moving so fast through the lake, that it leaves a wake behind like a boat. Some have said they have seen the monster crawl up onto the beach with **short flipper-like legs**. Once upon the sand, it holds its head high and turning it from side to side as it looks about.

In 1871- In the summer of 1871, a local citizen was said to have actually captured a "young" member of the monster family near Fish Haven. This report evidently had some credibility as it was reported in the Salt Lake City Herald:

"This latter-day wonder is said to be about twenty feet in length, with a mouth sufficiently large to swallow a man without any difficulty, and is propelled through the water by the action of its tail and legs."

In 1860 four people saw a large serpent-like creature, with about twenty feet visible, which appeared to be **covered in short hair**. They could also see **two of its flippers**.

One Account- A Mr. McNeil said that he saw a large creature **resembling an alligator** come on shore. He said it was a about **seventy-five feet long** and had a **horse-like head**.

Sometime before 1883 a group of men encountered a monster laying on the shore of the lake. Soon, the creature hurled itself into the water leaving a great commotion.

2002 Account- Captain Hirschi reported that in 2002 he saw a **sixty-five foot long monster** from about two-hundred yards. The Legend Of The Bear Lake Monster

1868 Account- The story was written by Joseph C. Rich and was sent to the Deseret News Newspaper. It goes as follow:

"The Indians have a tradition concerning a strange, serpent-like creature inhabiting the waters of Bear Lake, which they say carried off some of their braves many moons ago. Since then, they will not sleep close to the lake. Neither will they swim in it, nor let their squaws and papooses bathe in it. Now, it seems this water devil, as the Indians called it, has again made an appearance. A number of our white settlers declare they have seen it with their own eyes. This Bear Lake Monster, they now call it, is causing a great deal of excitement up here. S. M. Johnson at South Eden was riding along near the Lake the other day when he saw something a number of yards out in the lake which he thought was the body of a man. He waited for the waves to wash it in, but to his surprise, found the water washed over it without causing it to move. Then he saw it had a head and neck like some strange animal. On each side of the head were ears, or bunches the size of a pint cup. He concluded the body must be touching the bottom of the lake. By this time, however, Johnson seems to have been leaving the place so rapidly he failed to observe other details. The next day three women and a man saw a monstrous animal in the lake near the same place, but this time it was swimming at an incredible speed. According to their statement, it was moving faster than a horse could run. On Sunday last, N. C. Davis and Allen Davis of St. Charles; Thomas Sleight and James Collings of Paris, with six women were returning from Fish Haven when about midway from the latter place to St. Charles, their attention was suddenly attracted to a peculiar motion of waves on the water about three miles distant. The lake was not rough, only a little disturbed by the wind. Mr. Sleight ways he distinctly saw the sides of a very large animal that he would supposed to be not less than 90 feet in length. Mr. Davis doesn't think he was any part of the body, but is positive it must not have been less than forty feet in length, judging by the waves it rolled up on both sides of it as it swam, and the wave it left in the rear. It was going south, and all agreed it swam with a speed almost incredible to their senses. Mr. Davis says he never saw a locomotive travel faster, and thinks it made a mile a minute. In a few minutes after the discovery of the first, a second followed in its wake, but seemed much smaller, appearing to Mr. Sleight about the size of a horse. A larger one

152

followed this, and so on until before disappearing, made a sudden turn to the west a short distance, then back to its former track. At this turn Mr. Sleight says he could distinctly see it was of a brown color. They could judge somewhat of the speed by observing known distances on the opposite side of the lake; and all agree that the velocity with which these monsters propelled themselves, was astounding. They represent the waves rolling up on each side as about three feet high. This is substantially their statement as they told me. Messengers Davis and Sleight are prominent men, well known in the country, and all of them are reliable persons, whose veracity is undoubted. I have no doubt they would be willing to make affidavits to their statements.

In 1874, a traveler named John Goodman came through the Bear Lake Valley. He described an Indian legend about two lovers whom, upon being pursued by some of their fellow tribesmen, plunged into the lake and were changed by the Great Spirit into two large serpents. However, this is just a legend. The description of the Monster was the following: "*A creature with a brown-colored body, somewhat bigger in circumference than a man, anywhere from 40 to 200 feet long. Its head was shaped like a walrus without tusks or like an alligator's, and the eyes were very large and about a foot apart. It had ears like bunches, about the size of a pint cup. It had an unknown number of legs, approximately eighteen inches long, and it was awkward on land, but swam with a serpent-like motion at a speed of at least sixty miles an hour*". No one ever described the back part of the animal since the head and forepart was all that was ever seen. The rest was always under water.

Lake Champlain Monster

Lake Champlain has also been the site for a similar creature being seen. The first sighting was in 1609. The monster pictures have been published by Time and various other magazines. Champ has been featured on NBC TV's Unsolved Mysteries and Fox Network's Sightings, as well as on Japanese television and The Today Show. It has been the subject of books and hundreds of newspaper articles.

1977- Sandra Mansi photographed Champ while she was having a picnic with friends. This is the best known photograph of Champ..

Champ Video- As shown next -Something just under the surface of the lake that some say it is Champ. The video was taken by two fishermen with their digital camera in 2009. Before their supposed sighting, they were Champ skeptics. One of the fishermen said, *"It was as big around as my thigh. I'm 100 percent sure of what we saw. I'm not 100 percent sure of what it was."* The other one said, *"They never saw the entire body. What we saw always stayed at the surface and parts of it would come above the water, like the back of the nose or the head,"*

Other reported pictures of this popular monster are shown below.

154

Alaskan Sea Monster

The segment below is part of a fairly long video sequence of this monster. Travelling alongside a fishing boat, this monster made a substantial wake as it undulated past the boat and back into the Ocean.

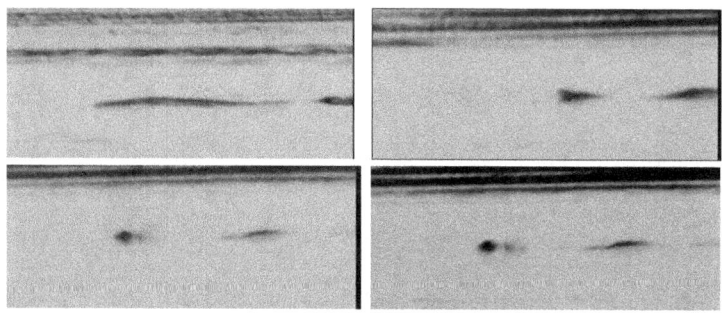

Lake Erie Sea Monster

Recently filmed, this sea monster is shown coming out of the water, showing its humps, swimming very fast with a massive wake and slowly going under as it approached the shoreline. I thought just the snap shots would give you a feeling of dread. If not re-read the story about the people being eaten in Florida.

Okanagan Lake Monster

Okanogan Lake "Ogopogo"-Canada has its own Plesiosauric monster named Ogopogo in the **Okanogan Lake**. This photo is from a movie film taken in August 1968 by Art Folden. The film shows three humps moving in the water.

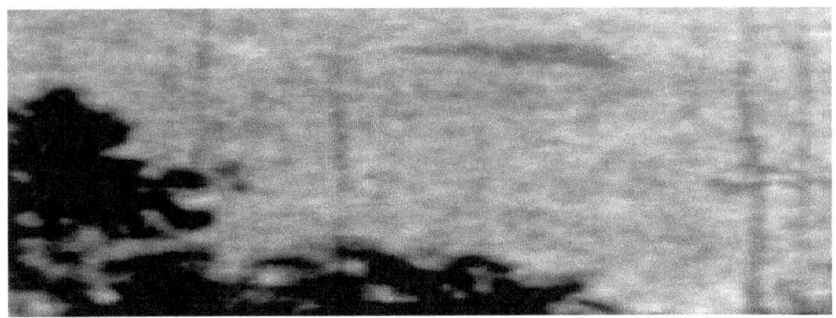

That isn't the only evidence as this thing has been seen many times as indicated by the pictures below.

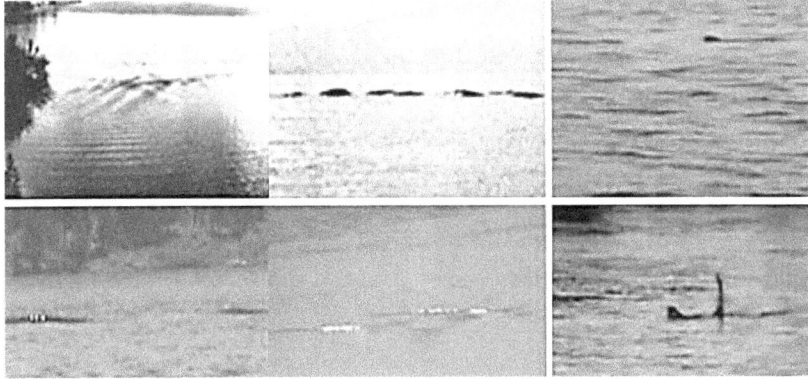

European Sightings

Water horse- While water-horse is an ancient Norse legend, there must have been some truth . The water horse is said to lure humans, especially children, into the water to drown and eat them. The water horse would encourage children to ride on its back. Its skin would become adhesive and the horse would drag to the bottom of the water

Norway Sea Serpent -This was a maned sea serpent was sketched in 1755 and found in *Natural History of Norway*.

HMS Plumber Sea Serpent -Presumed to be one of the pinniped variety, this drawing is from H.M.S. Plumper. Sketched by an officer on board, it was placed in the London News in 14 April 1849.[See above right]

Greenland Sea Serpent -A sea serpent reported by Hans Egede, Bishop of Greenland, in 1734 is drawn below. This looks to be one of the Cadborasaur versions. [Above left]

Early Pinniped Sea Serpent- Shown is an early rendering of a pinniped version of Sea Serpent. With its hairy face or mane. [Preceding right]

Merhorse Sea Serpent -Merhorse has been spotted around the world just about. It looks like a "maned serpent" reports, or a serpent with flippers and a horse's head.

Lake Lagarfljót Sea Serpent -This one is found in Iceland. The most recent sighting was in 1998, when a teacher and their class of pupils said they saw something close to the shore. Traditional sightings of this same lake monster go back to 1345. Somewhat snake-like it has a hump, a long neck, and whiskers, like a long-necked Water-horse. [Below left]

English Channel Sea Serpent-AMR is specifically requesting testimonials from anyone who might have recently seen something unexplainable in the English Channel. On April 20th, a French couple taking a stroll along the Bolounge Harbour managed to capture on film a dark, shape in the water. There have been a number of other independent reports of the same thing, all within the last couple weeks. In order to gather data, the AMR is asking for anyone who thinks they've seen something resembling a "fast-moving creature [Above right]

Skegness Beach Sea Monster

This popular tourist beach in the UK was the sighting spot for one of the monsters we have been talking about. This was not a Sperm whale like the one that was the talk of the town a few years ago. [Next left] Instead, This thing was serpentine, and made a similar humps show on the water surface, Even the tail was visible for a time. [See next right]

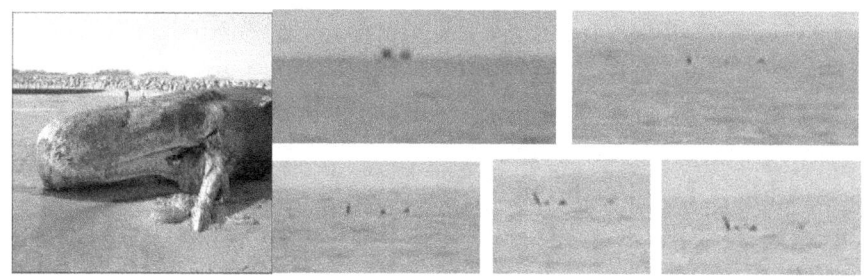

Morgawr Sea Monster

The Cornish coast is a place of rugged beauty but this place had a century old history about a giant sea beast. It was named Morgawr . Morgawr means 'sea giant' in the ancient, dialect of the Cornish people. The first documented sighting occurred in 1876. Fishermen though out nets and caught more than they were bargaining for. They discovered that they had caught a giant long necked beast. That fateful day Morgawr earned its status as more than just a legend. Images of the beast recently have been taken as shown left [some believe them to be the head of a swimming elephant..

Believed to be a dead Morgawr Sea Monster, a carcass was investigated and the picture above right] was taken. Two professors from Paris' Natural History Museum arrived at Querqueville to see if they could determine just what it was. When they departed, they took the monster's head and tail for comparison with museum specimens. They indicated the thing was not a whale and not a sea cow.

Italian Sea Serpent

A scientist named Ulysses Aldrovandus carefully described a small "monster" seen along a farm road in northern Italy which may have been the first tangible evidence we know. The date was

May 13, 1572. The poor, rare creature was so little that the farmer killed it just by knocking it on the head with his walking stick. The animal had done nothing wrong but hiss at the farmer's oxen as they approached it on the road. The scientist obtained the dead body and made measurements and a drawing. He even had the animal mounted for a museum. It had a long neck, a very long tail and a fat body. The skeletons of a number of ancient reptile-like creatures have similarities to this basic description. Drawings of his monster have been shown everywhere. Some samples are below. Most likely, the thing walked mostly on its fore legs out of the water and it appeared to be one of the many sea serpents seen throughout the years.

England's Nessie

Mar Lake "ness monster" has been spotted seven times. Known as the "bow-ness monster, it takes its name from a town on Windermere Country's northern. Luckily, the lake monster has been caught on video to prove the existence of England's monster.

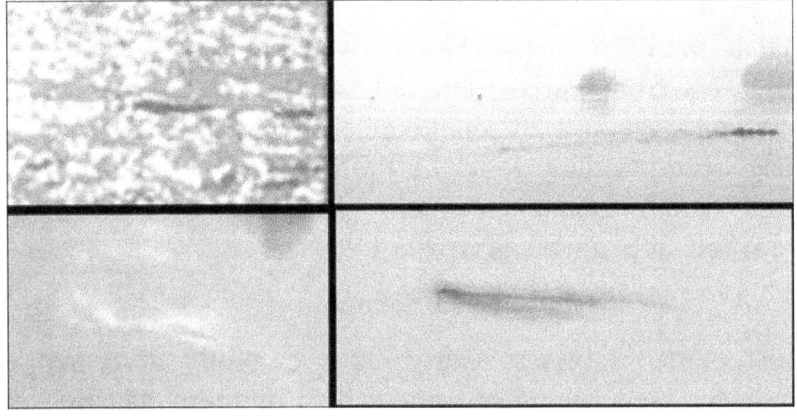

Ocean Nessie

The underwater photograph following was taken during the Jumble Trench expedition. This is just one of a number of photographs taken by the remote explorer in the trench, located in the North Sea, off the coast of Scotland. These convincing photographs of what many believe to be the Loch Ness monster, did not make the press. It is believed that a band of palaeontologists, fearing the effects of such evidence on their careers removed all traces of the expedition findings and burned all of the photographs. This one photograph was overlooked by the group, having been in the pocket of Clabby von Clabby, the head of the expedition. [Below left].

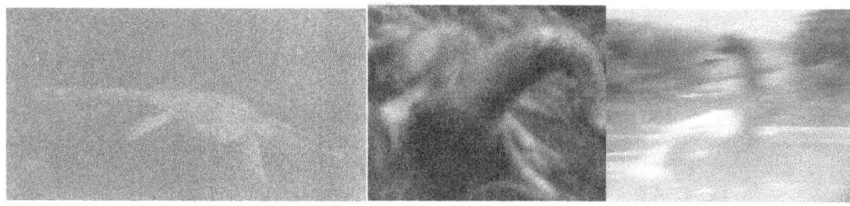

Sicily Monster

During a commercial holiday expedition in the Forests of Palermo, Italy, a number of holiday makers experienced a brief encounter with what the local tribesmen call to this day, "the Serpent of Sicili". Mr Ben Grace told reporters: *"I remember the appauling skin of the creature, like papier mache draped over a chiken wire frame"* The experience caused him to become a paleontologist. The animal quickly submerged after the flash of the first photograph, pictured below left. Another documented sighting in the area was that a man's hat was snatched by the toothy mouth of the monster as he strolled alongside the lake. [See the last 2 images above]

Loch Ness Monster

This guy must be the most famous "not quite captured" monsters of them all. The following sequence was filmed in 2002.

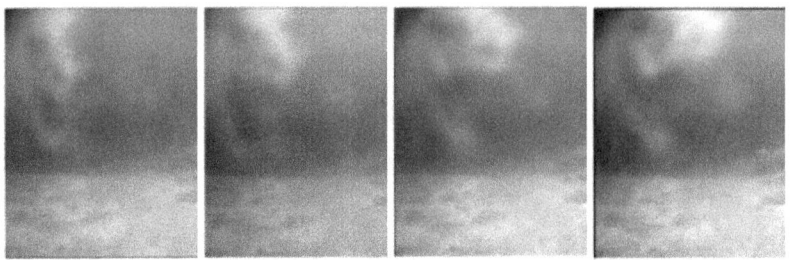

Another sequence was filmed in 2012 as the thing came really close to a small boat..

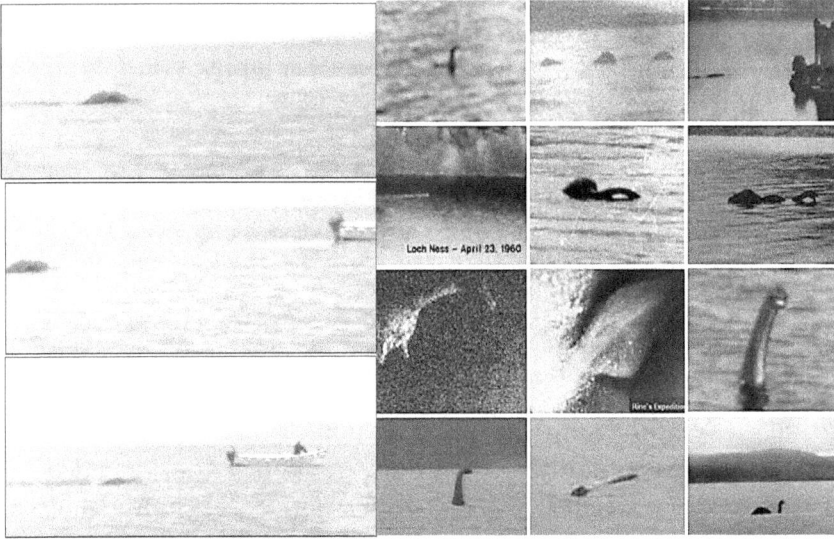

This monster has been the most talked about, filmed and documented of all sea serpents in the world. The collage of the more famous photos is shown above right.

April 19, 1934 - The most famous photo was taken by Colonel Robert Wilson. Christain Spurling later admitted that he had taken part in a hoax that allowed the picture to be taken. The picture is the first on the collage.

July 29, 1955- Bank manager Peter MacNab snapped a photo of something large moving through the water of the loch near Urquhart Castle.

In 1960--Aeronautical engineer Tim Dinsdale filmed a hump crossing the water in a powerful wake unlike that of a boat . JARIC declared that the object was "probably animate". In 1993 the film was enhanced to show another hump and possible fin of the monster.

Early 1970s - Frank Searle took an enormous number of photos of Nessie, many of which have been dismissed by experts as fakes.

1972- A photo taken seems to show the Loch Ness Monster moving toward the right with its hump protruding well above the surface and its mouth open.

1973-An underwater photo taken during the Rines expedition, seems to show a plesiosaur-like creature.

August 7, 1972- An expedition to find Nessie led by Dr. Robert Rines of the Academy of Applied Science struck gold when its underwater camera took a picture of what appeared to be the flipper of a large aquatic animal resembling a plesiosaur.

May 21, 1977- Anthony 'Doc' Shiels took the famous Muppet picture [bottom left of collage] while camping beside Urquhart Castle.

1970s- A 55 year old English lab technician captured the most compelling evidence for the existence of the fabled Loch Ness Monster in history, according to him. He said, of his short video "I couldn't believe my eyes when I saw this jet black thing, about 45- long, moving fairly fast in the water."

Asian Sightings

Chinese Sea Serpent-Thie ancient artwork below left shows what is believed to be ond of the Cadborasaur variety of Sea Serpent.

 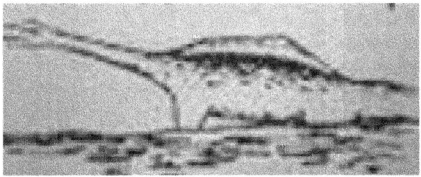

Lake Khaiyr Sea Serpent – [Above right]Similar to the Vorota monster, the Khaiyr beast is found in Northern Russia and is feared by the locals. The monster was seen on land by a member of a research team sent to look for it and it was grazing on the grass. It had a small head, longish neck, and a protruding dorsal fin. It was seen again by the team who thought it similar to the Vorota beast.

Lake Kokkol Sea Serpent -This Central Russian monster was seen by an archaeologist and his son. The kokkol creatures are large serpents said to dwell in various lakes in this part of Russia near Mongolia and China. Said to be immense serpents, perhaps 65 feet long, they inhabit cold lakes.

Lake Van Sea Serpent-Called Canavar, this one is found in Turkey. This creature has created quite the controversy of late since the Lake Van footage was taken. This shows an object, presumed to be the monster, swimming at great speeds through the lake. Then there is a close up of the beast's presumed head. A legend of a beast in the lake goes as far back as all written history of the region goes, and there is a depiction of the beast in an ancient engraving in an ancient church on one of the lake's islands. The canavar is said to bear triangular spikes on its back.

Lake Brosno Sea Serpent -Called Brosnie, this monster lives in Lake Brosno about 250 miles north west of Moscow Mentioned in local folklore dating back to at least 1854, "Brosnie" is thought to be similar to a dragon. A photo of the beast shows a panoramic view of the lake with a shining object near the front. One witness drew a sketch of what she saw, showing a big snake-like head with an eye on the side. [Depiction below left]

Lake Vorota Sea Serpent – [Above right]Vorota beast lives in Lake Vorota and a couple of nearby lakes in Siberia. The closest village is 100 miles away so very few people ever visit the lake. Expeditions have been sent to look for the Vorota beast and a number have seen the creature. It is described as being about 35 feet long, with a head 7 feet wide with widely separated eyes. It was grey in color and had a dorsal fin about 3 feet high, being shaped like the fin of a shark or porpoise. It was said to move "in a jumping manner" like a porpoise. Some just saw "humps" on the surface.

Lake Tianchi Sea Serpent- China has a mysterious lake monster, in fact there are several of them in Lake Tianchi. Lake Tiachi is in the mountains near Nepal. Besides just seeing the thing, it attacked 3 people one day and had to be driven back to sea. Additionally it evidently likes to eat cattle and sheep. Some have stated that the monsters have reached lengths of about 100 feet long. There have been numerous pictures and videos taken of these strange creatures one of which are below.

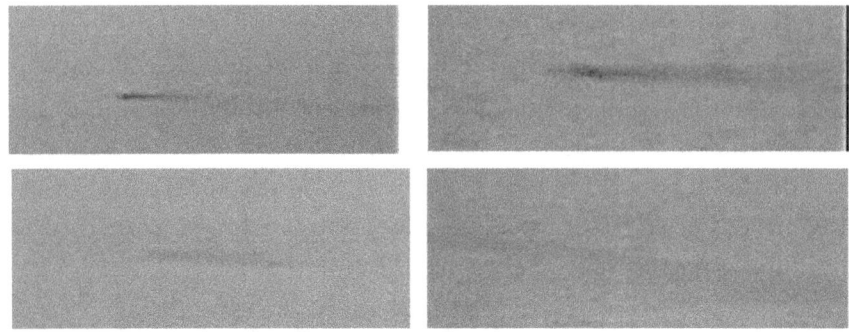

Vietnam Sea Serpent -This one is called Con Rit which means millipede. This snakelike monster washed ashore on a Vietnam beach in 1883. The monster was 60 feet long and 3 feet wide as depicted in the drawing- below left.

African Sighting

South African Sea Monster -In 1848, a sighting by several officers on the HMS Daedalus caused a sensation. The Daedalus was sailing near the Cape of Good Hope when the monster was seen. The visible part of the creature measured more than 60 feet, but only seemed to be 15 inches in diameter. Its color was dark brown and had some sort of mane. Drawing of the sighting is shown –above right]

Lake Van Turkey Sea Monster

The 'Lake Van monster' is the same type creature. Lake Van is the country's largest lake and even the provincial deputy governor claimed to have seen it. To the right is a frame from a home movie that got the animal. Possibly its eye.

Chinese Monster

China has its plesiosaur called the Lake Tianchi Monster. According to those who have seen it, the monster has a head somewhat like a human's, except with big round eyes, a protruding mouth and a neck about 3-1/2 feet long. It also has a white ring separating its neck and torso and smooth, gray skin. As many as 20 of the creatures were spotted swimming in the lake, which is in the Changbai mountains near the Korean border. The 2 pictures following are just a couple of the pictures taken.

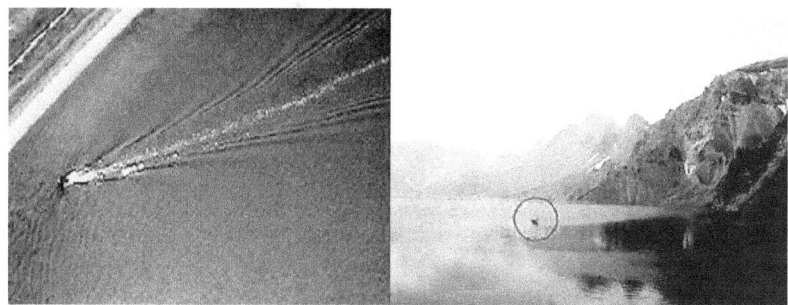

South American Sightings

Lake Lacar Sea Serpent -Named Cuero this monster is one of the few well-known South American lake monsters. Cuero means "cow-hide", and its back resembles a cow's hide. It also has a smooth head and strange tracks are often found around the lake, as well as the remains of eaten animals.

Nahuel Huapi Lake Sea Serpent -The creature of Nahuel Huapi Lake in Argentina and Patagonia is called Nahuelito. The story of this guy first attracted press coverage in the 1920s, though sightings date back well into the 19th century. Two pictures are shown below.

Argentina's "Nahuelito". -Many tourists around the popular resort of Bariloche have sighted a lake monster that has been dubbed "Nahuelito." Nahuelito is named after the body of water that is her domain, Nahuel Huapi Lake, which covers 318 sq. miles at the foot of the Patagonian mountains. Nahuelito has occasionally been visible for several minutes on the surface of the lake and has been sighted by scores of tourists and locals. Descriptions have varied from that of a giant water snake with humps and fish-like fins to a swan with a snake's head, the overturned hull of a boat, and the stump of a tree. Estimates of the creature's length range from 15 to 150 feet.

The Wye Monster

The photo below of an alleged plesiosaur was taken on 24th February 1996 by a Mr Hughie Miller, of Ross-on-Wye by a lakeside. This is what he said about the massive beast. *"It was huge, just massive, I can't recall ever seeing anything so big! I was in so much shock that it wasn't until the beast began sliding away on its belly that I remembered my camera! But as I pressed the shutter, I slipped on a slippy rock - I'm just lucky to have any evidence of my encounter I guess. It was fast for a big blue plastic replica".* I know this is odd, but I put it in just for completeness.

Basilosaur/ Plesiosaur

This type of sea monster is similar to the Cadbalosaur but larger in the belly portion, and it has 4 flippers rather than the pronounced 2 flippers of the Cadbalosaur. Bodies of the beast have been found all over. It also makes fewer humps in the water as it is slightly less snake like.

Japanese Plesiosaur-The picture below left is of one of the monsters was pulled in by a Japanese fishing ship. It was eventually tossed overboard from the smell, but its shape was well recorded.

Russian Plesiosaur-In Russia another Plesiosaur washed up to show that they are still around. [See preceding right]

Lukwata- Lukwata is found in the African Great Lakes. It is a very large snake-like animal. Said to be a large carnivorous serpent, it is feared by the natives when it makes a loud booming roar. One story says a native on a ships sailing in Lake Victoria was plucked from the bow. It has a small head on a body which slowly gets larger as it moves towards the middle.

How Many Plesiosaur-like Animals Still Exist?

According to different sources there are 250 or more different sightings of this type of creature around the world. Whatever these things are, they certainly seem to be relatives of the plesiosaur and at least some of them seem to be real. Speaking of real, do you think that dragons were real? Ancient texts seem to believe in them. It would have been almost impossible for them to have been on the Arc with Noah, but we can go to the Bible for proof of the post Babel Dragons.

If they did exist and simply appeared after the world-wide flood, then the most logical reintroduction method would have been genetic manipulation. Let's not concern ourselves about how they got here. Let's just look as a small fraction of the enormous amount of evidence that they were here "fairly recently". What we find is that, not only was this hot-breath creature reintroduced; it was greatly feared. Also evidence of smaller versions of the once great dinosaurs has been seen since the flood.

Californian Plesiosaur-In the United States we seem to find the remains every once in a while. A Plesiosaur-like specimen washed ashore in Monterey Bay, California in 1925. It sported a twenty foot long neck and long body. Its head is shown next left].

Yarru Monster

In Australia there are many stories and legends of dragons, with descriptions fitting dinosaurs, supporting that man and dinosaur did in fact live together. Australian aboriginal folklore abounds with such stories, including references to plesiosaur-like creatures. Elders of the kuku Yalanji aboriginal tribe of Far North Queensland, Australia, relate stories of Yarru, a creature which used to inhabit rain forest water holes. The painting shown above right depicts a creature with features remarkably similar to a plesiosaur. It even seems to show guts, indicating that these animals had been hunted and butchered.

Mosasaur/ Kronosaur

This type sea monster is almost crocodilian. Might jaws can snap its prey. Just think about a 90 foot crocodile. Some possible dead Mosasaur are shown below.

Rangoon Monster-The washed up corpse of an unknown monster [shown below] caused a fright for residents of the small port town of Viashino in Rangoon. The monster has been dubbed the Dragon draconis or 'Bert'. The new specimen is estimated to weigh almost 9000 pounds. The remains were returned to the ocean, it is unsure whether the residents of Rangoon will miss Bert.

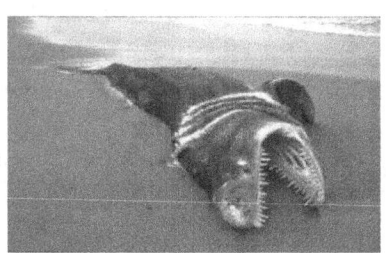

Lake Labinkir Sea Serpent -This one has been reported since the 60s as an aggressive monster in Lake Labinkir in Siberia. It certainly is carnivorous and has eaten a dog and a number of birds as others watched. People have seen the beast's neck rising from the lake as it made a sound similar to the cry of a baby. Other witnesses saw the beast swimming beneath the lake ice, and said it was lizard-like. [Drawing shown below left]

Lake Seljordsvatnet Serpent -Seljord serpent, also known as Selma, is found in Lake Seljordsvatnet in Norway. This creature has much evidence for its existence. This creature is described as crocodile-like, apparently having an elongate body and four small limbs. The Seljord serpent has been observed not only as an adult, but also as a baby; a small lizard-like animal. One 'baby' was killed by a housewife washing her clothes in the lake, but no one thought to examine the creature. It has also been observed on land, and one land sighting told of tiny front legs directly below the head. Possible image is shown above right.

Lake Storsjon Sea Serpent -Storsjoodjuret is found in and around Lake Storsjon Sweden. This creature is a large lake beast, described as crocodile-like, except it is said to have very large hind limbs with which it swims and tiny front limbs which dangle just beneath its head. This creature has been hundreds of reports since the mid-1600's. Many land sightings confirm that the creature moves in a strange undulating fashion. One witness thought that the creature had to have been a cross between a mammal and a fish. The beast is also said to raid crops planted near the lake, and to be dangerous to people. There have been reports of ears on the beast, almost always held down flat against its neck. The image below left is one of the sightings.

Bear Lake Monster - First sighting of the Bear Lake Monster was in 1868. A Mormon colonizer wrote a series of articles with claims that locals had seen a monster. It is described as a large crocodile creature. A local business owner claimed to have seen two hump above the surface of the water in 2002. According to another, the dark slimy monster surfaced right next to his boat. The Monster is said to be 90 feet long from end to end with a serpent like body and a face of a walrus as shown above right].

World War I Sea Serpent -In July 1915, the British steamer *Iberian* was shelled, and sunk off the coast of Ireland, The Submarine responsible say a massive sea Serpent come out of the water as the ship sank. Characterized as having 4 webbed feet, and 65 feet long, with a long tapered snout and tail [almost crocodilian], this monster sounds very familiar as shown below left.

Dobhar Chu – [Above right]A legendary creature that is said to inhabit the lakes of Ireland, that is reported to have killed people.

Massachusetts Monster-In 1970, another 50 foot long specimen washed up in Massachusetts as shown below.

Cornwall Sea Serpent-On Prah Sands in Cornwall a headless one of these creatures washed on shore. The remaining piece was 30 feet long. It had 4 small flippers and a tapered tail

Scottish Sea Serpent-Off Ayrshire, Scotland, in 1953 a 35 foot long animal with a long giraffe-like neck washed up on the beach. The smell got so bad, the villagers burned the carcass, but the description seems clear.

Live Monsters-There have been over 3000 sightings of that particular animal and similar creatures have been spotted on Lake Champlain and in Falmouth Bay, England.

Big Head Mosters

There is one more classification I wish to identify and show. I call it the big head, but it is snakelike and monstrous.

Swedish Big Head Monster

Here is one of the "Big Head monsters caught on film in the oceans of Sweden. These segments of a recent filming clearly show a massive head and long tail, What is was is a mystery, and thankfully, no one found out much about the huge head.

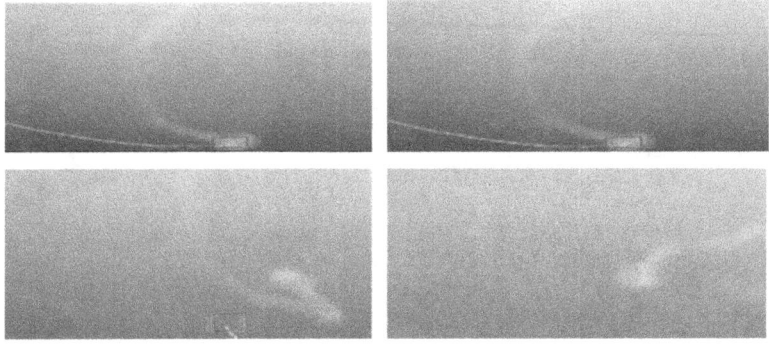

Japanese Big Head Monster

Apparently the same type of monster was seen in Japan. Segments of this video are shown below. Clearly the same type monster, its huge head and long tail were menacing. The boat at the top right of the images show how very large this thing was. One would think it could swallow the boat in one gulp.

Iceland Big Head Monster

The same big head monster showed up in Icelandic waters. The immense head and long tail are almost identical to the other 2 sightings. Just how many of these things are out there is not known, but they are being spotted frequently.

I know these things look like giant tadpole, but I would not get near the mouth part. We can believe that some of these sightings were mis understood or even made up, but the huge quantity of sightings and with many of those reporting being we recognized researchers, we must believe there are monsters out there. Another thing we know is that scientists today are working hard to make some more.

Monsters Being Designed

Just like was done in the Tertiary and Pleistocene Ages, we are now regenerating DNA modified animals at an alarming rate. As a clue, we are now seeing piglets with human faces. [See below]

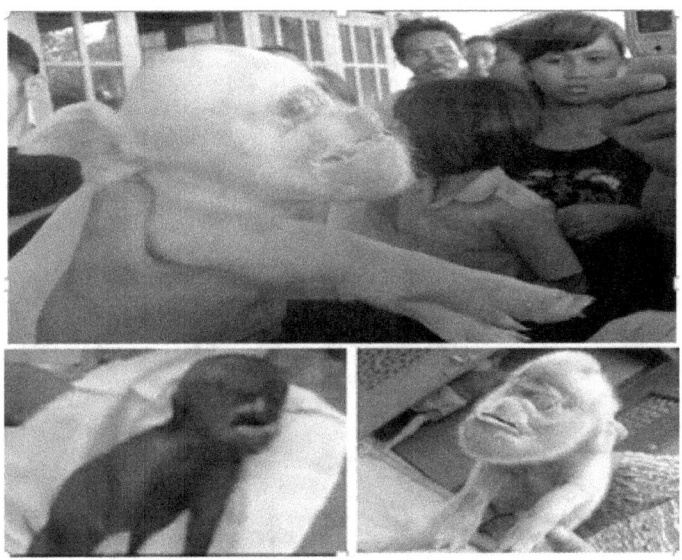

These are not made by inappropriate sexual conduct, but by something called Transhumanism. Possibly this trans-humanism was what happened during the Bharata War. Too much experimenting and not enough control has started to become an epidemic. It was initiated for a somewhat noble idea that we could make human parts on animals and only kill animals to keep us alive longer. It wasn't started until 1926 when Russian scientists began inseminations of chimpanzees in Africa and in Russia. We are told the experiments were unsuccessful. Since then gene spicing has become a household word.

Genetic Manipulation

Today scientists are much more responsible in what they do about making new animals. Most of us have heard about the puppies, fish, cats, and mice built to glow in the dark [1 and 2 in collage]. Others of the more responsible experiments include the fruit-fly grown to have legs coming out where antenna were [3], featherless chickens [4], big eared pigs and those with human organs [5], a human ear growing out the back of a mouse [6], gigantic animals like the monster bull [7], the sheep born with a human head [8], the mouse implanted with "created" memories [9], the dog with a second dog torso "bonded" to it.[10].

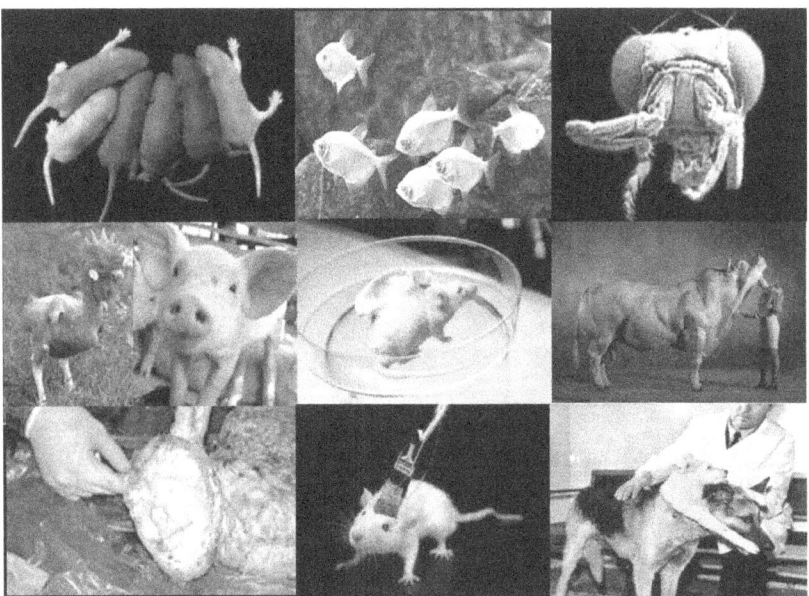

I just saw in the news England has granted it's OK to modify human genes to make a better baby, and we now have made an animal that is about 40% human to allow retrieval of body parts. While all of this seems well regulated and scientific and all, just imagine where the Pleistocene scientists went with it as they even recreated entire Tyrannosaurus Rex, just like the Jurassic Park movies.

Both genetic and just plain weird manipulation of our bodies has occurred recently. From the current events, we can only imagine what freaks were made before the time of Adam. Greeks tell us of half human half-goat people and many others. Today we have made all types of wonderful monsters. You may remember seeing a fruit-fly that had a second pair of wings coming out where his eyes or the animal that eats oil in some class at college, but it has become so much worse. As an update to the animal that eats oil, it was never let free in the environment because everyone was afraid of what it might also do. Many "mistakes" were done that we don't know about, I'm sure. Images below left are the pictures of genetically altered puppies that glow in the dark and a mouse with an unusual ear growing out of his back, but we didn't stop there, because nakedness was on our minds.

Genetically Bred Nakedness

We are not talking about people here, but instead we get naked chickens. [See the last picture] These genetically engineered chickens grow faster in hot climates, contain less subcutaneous fat to hold the feathers, require less ventilation in the summer, and are cheaper to produce because they don't require plucking. [Oh yes did I mention they're ugly?]

 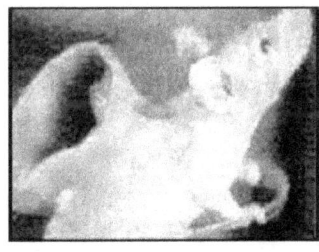 

Pig Grows a Heart

Naked chickens are OK, but can we produce replacement organs? Today, Italian scientists have modified DNA to make a pig grow a human heart. Let's not get too worried, but remember, according to ancient texts around the world, God killed almost everyone during the heaven wars and again killed almost everyone before the worldwide flood. One of the main reasons during both instances was that each group started making their own creations. That is not to say that if we quit researching genetics that meteors won't hit us and wars won't happen, it only means that history repeats itself and the genetic breeding is a confirmation of the repeating.

Mouse Grows a Kidney-If pigs can do it, so can mice. The Israeli's copied the Italians and made a mouse grow a miniature human kidney by introducing stem cells. The kidney produced urine and the whole bit. It was just tiny. Researchers in the UK saw what the Israelis were doing and grabbed some rats to see what they could do. Now they have modified a rat to grow a larger brain. Anyone who has seen the Pinky and the Brain cartoons knows what will happen with these guys, but now it's not a cartoon.

Almost a Human-I read recently that these crazy scientists can now make an animal that is 15% human. They taut it as a great accomplishment, but I'm not too sure. There is no greater warning from ancient religious and historical texts than the warning against changing animals into other animals.

Glowing Rat Hair-In the United States, scientists said, "We can do something with those rats!" They mixed tropical fish and jellyfish DNA into mice DNA to make mice hair glow green, red, or blue. That was pretty good, but one scientist said, "Let's turn them into robots."

Remote Control Rodents-As shown below, electrodes implanted into the brain and a remote control, force this rat to turn left, right, climb a tree, jump, and stop on command.

Just think what the scientific community has in store for people.

Mechanical Brain Transplant

We don't have brain transplants YET, but in March 2003 prototypes of the world's first brain prosthesis; an artificial hippocampus, was revealed to the public. By using this electronic device, scientists believe that defects that come from stroke, epilepsy or Alzheimer's disease may be treatable. The device simply reads information the brain normally sends to the hippocampus and it then sends out signals similar to those generated in the hippocampus. It's sort of a drop in replacement. It will not only affect memory but also a person's mood, awareness and consciousness. It will make a "new person" and how much difference there will be is not known. The bioengineering cyberneticists hope it will be a better person and I do to. That hippocampus is a strange word isn't it? I'm glad God didn't make a mistake and put a hippopotamus in our brain. I also hope the geneticists don't make that mistake.

Modern Chimera-Genetics

Those are just a very few of the genetic manipulated events. Our modern genetic magic is truly amazing. Here are a few more of the thousands of genetic manipulated successes.

- *Manufactured tobacco that produces human blood components.*
- *Manufactured tooth decay bacteria that won't cause tooth decay*
- *Manufactured gene that eliminates muscular dystrophy in mice*

- *Created cardiomyopathic mice so they could try to cure this human only disease*
- *Manufactured skin that was transplanted onto 45% of a baby's bad skin.*
- *Manufactured worms that live 50% longer than others.*
- *Genetically altered blind dog that could see again*
- *Genetically altered sightless fish that now have eyes*
- *Produced bone from skin and gum tissue*
- *Genetically engineered ears on mice*
- *Developed an artificial drug that burns fat faster in mice*
- *Altered hair to make it glow different colors*
- *Genetically altered rabbit that glows under a black light.*
- *Genetically grown frog eyes and frog ears without a frog*
- *Genetically grown snake venom cells without a snake*
- *Produced a mouse with downs syndrome*
- *Altered a fish that grows faster, mates more often and his offspring that dies more quickly, showing that genetically manufactured animals could accidentally wipe out species.*

If that list is impressive, those are only a few of the things we know about. We can assume where there are a few successes, there are many mistakes. This list does show that cloned and manufactured animals and control of genetics are both becoming common place in something we call Trans-human Chimera.

Transhumanism

Transhumanism is modern genetic modification of humans. Since 2011 DARPA has provided millions of dollars in this type of bio-design to increase capabilities in soldiers. Add gorilla strength, cheetah speed etc. The one they are currently interested in is soldiers with genetic night vision like some of the deep sea animals. This goes way beyond what we imagined. We are used to genetically modified crops and drugs to cure cancer, but this is something else. In Britain, for instance, you can have a fetus developed to a specific sex, eye color and other capabilities. It's like getting a store bought baby. At one time this sort of thig must have gone too far. One report indicates Britain alone there were over 150 "fully developed" animal/human chimeras in 2012. Let me show you some of the success that may be already done. Here is a cute bunny with human features. This Chimera was made in South America and filmed in 2011. Next to her is a frog-human chimera developed in 2010.

 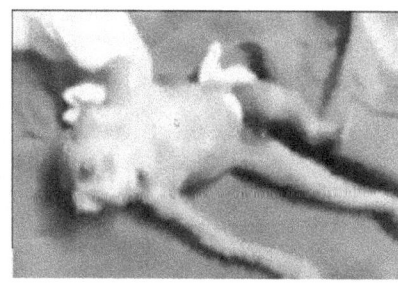

A German museum reportedly hatched a Gasosaurus theropod egg found in China that is supposedly still alive. [See next left]. In New Zealand they are attempting to clone a 100 year old Tasmanian Tiger fetus preserved in alcohol. [Next right]

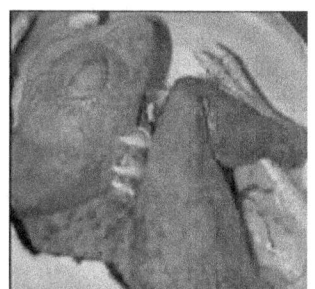 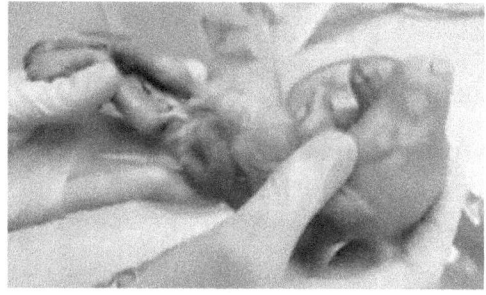

Don't even belive that some science experiment gone wrong did not make a huge population of Ape-like humans or throw backs to dinosaurs. Here is something else to wonder. How close are we to doing it today? Today, we are attempting to create all type of animals just like the ANAK. Last time that was done, God flooded the entire world. What will happen this time?

Conclusions

You read the whole book and I'm very glad. I know that the concepts presented were weird at best, but keep an open mind. Hopefully you will not dismiss the sightings of these miraculous, often dangerous animals. I tried to provide you with, not only the possibility, but also a reasonable method for their developments.

Ancient civilized people lived during the Mesozoic Age and walked with dinosaurs. They had an advanced civilization and most likely made massive animals from the normal sized ones of that time.

Ancient War Animals- I showed you the details about the dinosaur and dinosaur like animals that were specifically created for action in the Heaven Wars that ended with the Cretaceous Extinction.

Shortened Timeline- Now that we know Nuclear decay is not constant, other timing methods show that the Cretaceous extinction was only about 120 thousand years ago.

ANAK people- Hopefully I presented enough detail about these rulers of the world. These people lost the Heaven Wars, but they controlled the Earth for thousands of years. In that time they did not stop creating animals. God called them the UNCLEAN ANIMALS. Some of the texts were even more derogatory about how the ANAK and those that were trained by them destroyed the initial animal genetics to create a {BETTER} group.

Remanufactured Monsters- Soft tissue in dead dinosaurs can only mean they were alive until recently or during the Pleistocene.

The Pleistocene Worldwide Flood- Hopefully you understand that this worldwide flood was not only initiated to kill all the people, but also all the unclean animals.

After the Flood- We examined how other cultures weathered the storm. The Sumerians tell us that some stayed in flying ships and cried out to the Lord as they were deathly afraid of the evidence of his wrath.. Finally the storms subsided and the entire world was repopulated much too quickly according to almost all scientists. . The only practical observation to make is that the animals were recreated around the world. These included many, many UNCLEAN animals and some of the varieties we have identified in this book. Relics of the dinosaur age and monsters of all varieties roamed the earth .

ANAK Stayed young- To control the world the ANAK had to stay young. Evidence that they had some method to stay young is indicated everywhere. 1 presented some of the images that might have shown the Live extensions noted by these rulers known as gods.

Tower of Babel War- 6 thousand years ago, another huge war almost destroyed the earth. With it, the capabilities of many people was changed. The knowledge of the ancient pre flood past had been lost. ANAK began to get old and their descendents [half ANKA and half "normal human" demi-gods took control for a period of time. These guys had long skinny heads, they were large, they had 2 rows of teeth and 6 toes per foot, but they were basically normal humans.

Ape-men- Some of the people lost more than memory- they became like apes. So much evidence is around, it is hard to believe anything else. It was these ape people who may have been the ancestors of the Ape-men seen around the world today. Hundreds of these ape-people have been seen around the world as evidence of their existence.

Plesiosaurs- The Bible called them Leviathan. Many types of sea serpents continued to live after the flood and war. Hundreds have been seen and some have even been eaten getting too close to these monsters.

Smaller Dinosaurs- Without a doubt, large land animals with characteristics of the ancient dinosaurs were recreated by the

ANAK using some type of genetic manipulation. Today, many are trying to see if there are some of these creatures still alive.

Flying Reptiles- Even very recently, we have photographic, and eye witness accounts of these dangerous monsters.

Giant Kraken- Today the mystery of the Kraken has been reduced as many have seen, and touched these things. Mostly they die if they try to fight one of today's ships, but be careful in a smaller sailing vessel.

Huge Snakes- These like the other monsters are still around. 60 foot ones are not that uncommon and that is 6 stories high if it was pulled upward. Eating bulls, and even people, these were part of the miscreated animals of the ANAK.

Today, we are attempting to create all type of animals just like the ANAK people. Last time that was done, our creator got really angry.

The End!

About the Author

Steve Preston is a long time author of scientific, esoteric facts. His series on the creation of mankind is shown below. The series focuses on the painful truths rather than whitewashed details that make us comfortable. If you are interested in the truth instead of comfort, please continue to read and, while you are at it, review other works by Mr. Preston as shown below.

Four Part Series "Vibrational Matter"

Vibrational Matter

10-Dimentional Universe

Walk Though a Wall and Time

The Meaning of Light, Life, and Death

Live and Die the Right Way [Addendum]

Eight Part Series "History of Mankind"

The First Creation of Man

The Second Creation of Man

The Creation Of Adam And Eve

The Antediluvian War Years

Man After the Flood

Life After the Babel War

A New View Of Modern History

The 20th Century To The End Of Time

Living Underground

Truth Series

The Truth About Dinosaurs

The Truth About The Earth

The 7 Destructions of the Earth

The Truth About the Heaven War

Truth About Dinosaurs

Who Really Discovered the Americas?

God Didn't Make The Ape

Our Very Odd Presidents

Today's Monsters

 Truth About Vampires

Planet Series

When Did People Live on The Moon?

Evolution of the Planets

The Day Venus Exploded

Living on Mars

Odd Series

The Book Of Odd

More Oddness

Why Are There So Many Anomalies?

Stupid Science

Other Works

A Closer Look At Lincoln

Adam, Lilith, and Eve

America's Civil War Lie

Ancient History of Flying

Behind the Tower of Babel

The Funny Book of Law

When Giants Ruled the Earth

Lizard People

Religious Series

The Truth About Vampires

Self, Soul and Spirit

The truth About the Anakim Gods

A Closer Look At Genesis

Live and Die the Right Way

www.ingramcontent.com/pod-product-compliance
Lightning Source LLC
Chambersburg PA
CBHW071151290526
45788CB00001BA/378